THE
WRITER'S CRUSADE

THE
WRITER'S CRUSADE

KURT VONNEGUT AND THE MANY LIVES OF SLAUGHTERHOUSE-FIVE

TOM ROSTON

Abrams Press, New York

Library of Congress Control Number: 2021934857

ISBN: 978-1-4197-4489-1
eISBN: 978-1-68335-924-1

Printed and bound in the United States
10 9 8 7 6 5 4 3 2 1

ABRAMS The Art of Books
195 Broadway, New York, NY 10007
abramsbooks.com

To all peace-loving pilgrims who confront life's traumas with beauty and truth . . . and jokes.

If at the end of a war story you feel uplifted or if you feel that some small bit of rectitude has been salvaged from the larger waste, then you have been made the victim of a very old and terrible lie.

—TIM O'BRIEN

Everything was beautiful, and nothing hurt.

—KURT VONNEGUT

CONTENTS

CONTENTS

CHAPTER ONE

KURT VONNEGUT, NAZI SLAYER!

ALL THIS HAPPENED:

I really did begin research on this book in November 2018, and by November of the next year I made a remarkable discovery about Kurt Vonnegut. Or what appeared to be. I had tracked down Bernie O'Hare and interviewed him over the phone. He was talking on his Bluetooth headset while driving to Oneonta in upstate New York, and I was sitting on my living room couch in Brooklyn using a cordless phone attached to a digital recording device. I wanted to talk to Bernie about his father, Bernard V. O'Hare, because I had come to think that his dad may have had an even greater significance to 1969's *Slaughterhouse-Five* than its author, Vonnegut, had led us to believe.

Vonnegut and O'Hare had buddied up during World War II and had been captured together by the Germans during the Battle of the Bulge in December 1944 and put in a prison camp and eventually in a meat locker under a slaughterhouse, where they miraculously survived the Allies' devastating firebombing of Dresden. It was a turning point in Vonnegut's life, one that he documented in his famous novel, which took him twenty-three years to complete.

Most of this you probably already know because you've read his book. Vonnegut writes about this experience with O'Hare in

1

the first chapter of *Slaughterhouse-Five* as if it's nonfiction, but then the next nine chapters are about a fictional character, Billy Pilgrim, who travels in time and is abducted by aliens from the planet Tralfamadore, and whose war experiences loosely parallel Vonnegut's, all of which makes it *metafiction*, meaning it upends the conventional fictional narrative by blurring the line between the author and the story being told.

Vonnegut didn't even set that initial chapter apart by calling it a preface or an author's note. He just dropped himself into that first chapter and then sporadically throughout. I'd like to do that!

I wanted to know more about O'Hare because, despite there being reams of commentary about *Slaughterhouse-Five* by Vonnegut and others, there isn't a whole lot about this seemingly essential character, other than what Vonnegut writes in the book and what he mentioned occasionally in interviews and essays.

As a middle-aged freelance journalist and author of a couple of middling successful nonfiction books, I wanted my *Slaughterhouse-Five* book to break new ground on how people perceive Vonnegut's masterpiece, and I thought the path might be through O'Hare. I needed the money from writing the book, yes, and a groundbreaking book could result in more of it. But I also felt like I was running out of time to make my mark as a writer. So I went all out. I bought $255 tickets on Delta from New York to Vonnegut's hometown of Indianapolis, reserved a room at the Cascades Inn in Bloomington, Indiana, and made plans to visit the Lilly Library at Indiana University, where I wanted to dig into Vonnegut's discarded drafts of *Slaughterhouse-Five* to find a literary Holy Grail, some secret Da Vonnegut Code that no one had found before.

On the first day at the Lilly, a weird thing happened. While I sat in the spacious reading room with high ceilings and large wood tables, an older, heavy-set librarian crashed into a door that swung out at her and she quietly collapsed into a heap on the floor. One of her fellow librarians broke the silence by gasping, "Oh!" I got up from my chair, unsure if I should approach, but quickly sat back down as several other librarians gathered with hushed voices. Medics arrived and asked the woman if she knew what year it was. I believe she answered correctly before they rolled her out on a gurney.

I really enjoyed my time in Bloomington, eating breakfasts of yogurt, toast, and Square Donuts ("Never cut corners" is the local franchise's slogan) in the common area of the Cascades Inn, a nondescript white motel by the side of the road, which was also hosting an international group of ethnomusicologists who were gathering in the heartland for a conference at the university. The European and Latin American music geeks—I say this with affection—were mostly young graduate students dressed in scarves and wool sweaters, while the Americans were old enough to be their grandparents, dressed in fleece and L.L.Bean boots. Both seemed to be equally delighted to be there, talking excitedly about the merits of juice not from concentrate and string instrument esoterica while an electric heater with a digital fireplace display hummed nearby.

On the morning of my third day at the Lilly, I was putting my belongings in a locker as requested—they have more than Vonnegut's drafts to protect; the Lilly houses a first folio of Shakespeare, a first edition of *The Canterbury Tales,* and Spider-Man No. 1, among other relics—when the lights went out. It was totally dark in the locker area. I walked out of the room and I again witnessed librarians in a moment of crisis. They were as calm, swift, and organized as Austrians. Visitors and staff were led into a windowless common area where we were informed that the building would be closed for the day.

I pleaded with a head librarian that I had flown 750 miles to be there, but she remained firm and waited for me to stop talking. I wandered over to the nearby I. M. Pei–designed IU Eskenazi Museum of Art building, which had backup generators, so I sat and watched a troupe of dance students dressed in white leotards and lace perform a dance called "Ascension," in honor of the museum's reopening, up and down the stairs of the vast space. I occasionally walked over to the Lilly to see if the electricity was back on until the librarian and I worked out that I could return the following Monday before regular opening hours. I later found out that there was an oversurge at a nearby substation that had put most of the university campus in the dark until later that night.

I mention these moments to attest to how random, awkward, and fallible life can be. And how, when working on a book about Vonnegut, one becomes more mindful of such things because Vonnegut wrote books about life's strange rhythms, from the mundane to the horrific, in a way few other writers could. Perhaps he did it best in *Slaughterhouse-Five* when he writes, "So it goes," after each and every death, a phrase that became a slogan for a generation.

And so. Rifling through hundreds of typed pages, some with coffee stains and Vonnegut's scribbles, I saw that he had indeed tried to feature O'Hare in more prominent ways, including dedicating the entire book to him at one point, before he ultimately dedicated it to a German cabdriver, Gerhard Müller, and

Bernard's wife, Mary O'Hare, whom he credited for inspiring him to write the book in a way that would resist glorifying war by showing that it is, in fact, complete and utter tragedy and pain. After returning to New York, to further pursue my hunch about O'Hare, I searched for his and Mary's son Bernie. And it was Bernie who told me something new, something I'd never heard before, something, until now, that you've never heard before. Bernie said he once spoke to a Vietnam veteran who went out drinking with his father and Vonnegut and that the two World War II veterans had strongly intimated to the Vietnam vet that in the brief lull after they were liberated in 1945, they hunted down one of their sadistic German prison guards. Then they killed him.

Whoa.

I hope that we share the same shock at the implications of this information. After all, Vonnegut's actual war experience is what gave his legendary anti-war novel and subsequent activism such gravitas. The man saw the worst things that war can do! His combat experience is notable for its wretchedness and absurdity. Everyone knows that his biggest takeaway was that he witnessed an atrocity: the Allied bombing of Dresden, in which tens of thousands of German civilians were killed. The notion that the man who went on to espouse anti-violence and the Christ-like (if ironic) sanctity of kindness could have committed cold-blooded murder just doesn't seem credible.

Before I go any further into the possible veracity of O'Hare's story, I'll say right now, *I don't think it is true.* Wait, saying it in italics doesn't feel emphatic enough, so I'll say it in caps: I DO NOT THINK THIS STORY IS TRUE.

But, honestly, I *wanted* it to be true. I had a greedy feeling as I tried to verify the story. I knew that if I could prove it, the story would make my book explosive. And not only that, I got a buzz at the idea of a lanky, bookish writer type—yeah, maybe I was projecting myself in the role—committing vigilante justice against a cruel Nazi. I tracked down the guy Bernie was referring to, John Kachmar, a retired businessman and local politician, who was living in Bethlehem, Pennsylvania. After some phone tag, Kachmar called me from his car outside his house, where he sometimes sits to smoke a cigar.

This is what Kachmar told me:

In 1972, after a tour of duty in Vietnam and being discharged from the Marine Corps, Kachmar was a senior attending Moravian College in Bethlehem, and he was studying *Slaughterhouse-Five* for a creative writing class. While he was reading the book, being from Bethlehem, Kachmar recognized the name Bernard V. O'Hare as the local district attorney. He thought, *Maybe I could get a good grade if I interview O'Hare.*

Kachmar thumbed through the Yellow Pages and found O'Hare's number, called it, and asked if he could talk to him about *Slaughterhouse-Five.* He was flatly rebuffed. "Mr. O'Hare does not give interviews for the book," he was told.

Kachmar mentioned the story over the dinner table to his father, who said O'Hare was a friend of his and that he'd call him. O'Hare relented and Kachmar was in his office a couple days later.

It was an early afternoon when Kachmar sat across from O'Hare, surprised at what a small, skinny guy he was and what an enormous nose he had. O'Hare was a funny bird; he was known to mow his lawn dressed in a suit.

Almost immediately, Kachmar hit a wrong chord when he said that he understood why Vonnegut wrote about alien time travel in his book and how, if you were in combat, you could go back in time and almost smell things from your past.

O'Hare looked at him hard and snapped, "How the fuck would you know that?"

Kachmar stuttered and eventually explained that he had fought in Vietnam, been wounded, and been in a bad-luck unit that endured devastating casualties, particularly in Dai Do, a notorious three-day battle in 1968, where more than eighty Americans died.

O'Hare immediately apologized and the conversation turned into a four-hour ramble, during which O'Hare told Kachmar about his experiences in the war. The two men—O'Hare was over fifty and Kachmar was in his twenties at the time—shared how incoming artillery shelling terrified them and how they'd both lost their Christian faith after their war experiences.

And O'Hare told Kachmar that after he and Vonnegut were released, they had tracked down one of their guards. "And he left me with the distinct impression, if not the words, that they had killed the guard," Kachmar says. "Or at least roughed him up pretty bad."

About six weeks after the conversation, O'Hare called Kachmar and asked him if he wanted to meet a friend of his. Kachmar agreed to have a drink with O'Hare at a bar in Bethlehem, and when he got there he saw Vonnegut sitting with O'Hare. The two men proceeded to drink Kachmar under the table, and during the drinking they talked about war and Vonnegut asked Kachmar about his time in Vietnam.

It was not a fun night out. It was, "at best, morose," recalls Kachmar, who says that all three of them probably had some form of post-traumatic stress disorder (PTSD), but that Vonnegut seemed to have it the worst because he was so grim. The subject of the German guard came up again, but Kachmar didn't press the men for details. Both O'Hare and Vonnegut had vacant stares when they talked about it. "War is a horrible thing," Kachmar says. "It fucks you up." He believed that they were corroborating, without words, what O'Hare had told him weeks earlier. Neither men said the word "kill," but Kachmar is certain that they were telling him that they had hunted for the guard and eventually found him.

Kachmar was so drunk that the men left him on the ground outside his home, where his wife dragged him in. He was unsettled by the experience. Although Kachmar never saw Vonnegut again, he maintained a relationship with O'Hare for many years, but he never gleaned any more information about the German guard.

Although Kachmar is convinced that O'Hare and Vonnegut were telling him that they had been part of an act of vengeance, he is also clear that his memory is hazy and that they never actually said that they killed the guard.

I KNOW. That's not a lot to go on. So why am I willing to muddy the waters of our real world of rivers, gravitational pulls, and actual people who do actual things to each other by putting such a speculative story into print? Because this new tale—*Kurt Vonnegut, Nazi Slayer!*, for a time the working title for this book— opened a crack, a view into myself as a fan of *Slaughterhouse-Five* and, in turn, a new appreciation of the book's monumental significance today. I was convinced that I had been won over by the book's clear vision of war as repugnant, that I shared its abhorrence of conventional war stories, and that I believed that the trauma it represents is a calamity beyond measure.

But those ideals cracked at the whiff of Nazi blood. I pursued *Kurt Vonnegut, Nazi Slayer!* doggedly because I was thrilled by the fantasy of an emaciated, 22-year-old Vonnegut aiming down a rifle at the former Nazi guard who had treated him cruelly and, in a small way, avenging all the horror committed by the Third Reich. It was a story rich with drama, irony, and significance. And in the same way I have enjoyed watching many, many Nazis being blown away—or having their faces melted off—in a variety of movies, I got a kick out of the prospect of Vonnegut kicking ass.

My moral indignation had been superseded by a seductive narrative. I think most of us respond more to a story—a series of events that happen to a character that follows an arc with a beginning, middle, and end—than, say, just a principle or an isolated fact. That's why politicians are always casting their ideas or themselves within storylines. Stories are the way we comprehend the world around us. They are how we understand ourselves; we punch our collective experiences into recognizable storylines—struggling writer, pulled-up-by-her-own-bootstraps politician, unfairly treated younger sibling—that we codify as our identities.

And the revenge narrative is particularly beguiling. In the natural order, there are animals that avenge themselves to deter future attacks. But for humans, revenge also serves as one of the foundational organizing principles for civilization. The precept of "an eye for an eye" dates back to Babylonian times. And retributive justice was more than a way to create social order; it underlies how we thought the universe works.

The pre-Socratic Greek philosopher Anaximander wrote that the cosmos was governed by the settling of scores. He believed that the seasons function under that principle; the heat of summer has to pay for itself by the cold of winter, and so on.

Revenge can make us feel like there is order and fairness—that wrongs are righted, that we don't live in chaos.

That deep foundation underlies why we enjoy at least fictional violence; it's not something everyone wants to partake in, but I count myself as one of those who has moral qualms with murder and mayhem but also gets visceral pleasure, a dopamine rush, when I see it in a movie or TV show.

And, what's more, an effective revenge story usually hangs on a clear dichotomy of good versus bad—cigar-chomping American grunts against Nazis or resistance fighters against an intergalactic Evil Empire—in which a more powerful malevolent force gets its comeuppance in the end. That sort of clarity is more satisfying than the prospect that life is just really complicated or that random misfortune can dictate our lives and that the innocent can lose in the end because, you know, sometimes a substation goes out or a door hits you in the face or you get shelled by bombs one too many times.

And when you combine revenge with war, you get a double whammy of excitement, far from the rigmarole of our everyday lives, tales where the stakes are high and the lines are clear.

As Ernest Hemingway wrote in a letter to F. Scott Fitzgerald, "War is the best subject of all. It groups the maximum of material and speeds up the action and brings out all sorts of stuff that normally you have to wait a lifetime to get."

I never served in the military. Never been near a war zone. Instead, I have been raised on what movies tell me about war, from *Rambo* to *Platoon* to Quentin Tarantino's *Inglourious Basterds*, the latter of which gleefully depicts a troop of vengeful Nazi-killing Americans in World War II. I got my kicks watching that movie, just as I loved Hollywood classics (*The Great Escape*,

Saving Private Ryan) and muscular war novels (*For Whom the Bell Tolls, The Naked and the Dead*). For many like me, war is a dramatic tale starring Brad Pitt or Tom Hanks. In Vonnegut's day, it was John Wayne or Frank Sinatra. What distinguishes *Slaughterhouse-Five* from those narratives is that Vonnegut stayed true to the promise he made to Mary O'Hare to make war unappealing in every way. I have so much respect for that. But the *Kurt Vonnegut, Nazi Slayer!* story showed to me that I have a very hard time shaking my impulses. I would have to watch myself closely to see if I could fully appreciate, in my gut, that war is pain and that most war stories, including the ones I tell myself, are lies.

I sought out war veterans who could steer me away from romanticizing war. First on my contact list was Vietnam veteran Tim O'Brien, whose 1990 book, *The Things They Carried*, is arguably the most influential book about war from the past three decades. Indeed, it has been a helpful guide as I have looked at *Slaughterhouse-Five*, even if the two authors have very different writing styles. They still share the same fidelity to the ideal that war stories should be treated with vigilance and skepticism. But there is a direct earnestness to O'Brien's writing that provides a good foil to Vonnegut's lopsidedness. O'Brien is the straight man to Vonnegut's joker.

In the "How to Tell a True War Story" chapter of *The Things They Carried*, O'Brien writes, "In war you lose your sense of the definite, hence your sense of truth itself, and therefore it's safe to say that in a true war story nothing much is ever very true. Often in a true war story there is not even a point."

From a different angle, Vonnegut articulates a similar sentiment in the first chapter of *Slaughterhouse-Five* when he writes, "There is nothing intelligent to be said about a massacre." In the book, Vonnegut does not explicitly describe the horrors of war—the events themselves and the lasting trauma—but instead uses elision, misdirection, and irony to relay its devastation. In a later chapter, he muses that "Everything was beautiful and nothing hurt" would be a good epitaph for both himself and Billy Pilgrim. But we know that nothing could be further from the truth.

In order to strip anything redeeming from his story—be it pathos, glory, or moralizing—Vonnegut sought to implode the narrative process. Jerome Klinkowitz, a Vonnegut scholar who has written many books about the work by the author and is now a retired University of Northern Iowa professor, wrote in his *Kurt Vonnegut's America*, "*Slaughterhouse-Five* is principally a book about itself. About itself being written and itself being read." In other words, Vonnegut recognized that the war story itself had to be undone in order for it to be truthful.

By doing so, he provided a salve to war veterans, including himself. Not that he would have characterized the book's impact in such deliberate, do-good fashion. Instead, Vonnegut liked to crack that the only benefit from the Dresden massacre went to him—financially. "I wrote this book, which earned a lot of money for me and made my reputation, such as it is," he would say. "One way or another, I got two or three dollars for every person killed. Some business I'm in."

TO UNSTICK US FROM TIME A BIT, you should know that at the Lilly Library I eventually came upon one of Vonnegut's discarded versions of *Slaughterhouse-Five*, in which the American POW narrator recalls his 17-year-old Nazi guard. "He was a baby," Vonnegut writes. "I wonder where he is. Dead, I expect. There was a time when we promised to kill him."

Could this be a veiled confession? Not necessarily. It could more easily suggest that Vonnegut and O'Hare both tinkered with this myth as dark humor and that they had pulled Kachmar's leg with it. Still, it kept me on the trail. I talked about Kachmar's story with many people close to Vonnegut or who were knowledgeable about his experiences in the war. No one corroborated the tale.

I consider Brian Welke, a Florida judge who has taken on a side project researching Vonnegut's real-life Slaughterhouse Five unit, to be a strong source. Over close to ten years, he has spoken with more than sixty members of Vonnegut's 423rd Regiment along with the same number of their relatives, in addition to dozens of veterans from other units. Welke, a real straight arrow, describes his report as "the antithesis of *Slaughterhouse-Five*," because his is not a creative project but one purely based on historical documentation.

Welke says he specifically asked his sources if there were acts of vengeance. No one spoke of any. "I would be shocked if it were true," he says of Kachmar's German guard revenge story.

One of Bernie O'Hare's sisters, Theresa Wenck, tells me that she "highly doubts" the story. She thinks of her father, Bernard, and Vonnegut as extremely similar tempermentally, and she recalls how her dad refused to set mouse traps in their house, leaving the job of killing vermin to his wife. And he once told Theresa, "I probably would have lost my mind if I had to shoot somebody" in the war.

Vonnegut's three oldest children—Mark, Edith, and Nanette—agree that it doesn't have "the ring of truth," as Nanette says. Mark concedes that, "in a way, it would be dramatic and cool if he had done that," but, for one thing, none of his children saw their father as capable of committing an act of violence.

Nanette does have one vague memory of her father speaking of needing to be restrained during the war because he wanted to kill a particularly sadistic guard named "Junior," but she recalls it abstractly and maintains that the prospect is unlikely.

Edith adds that Kurt suffered from unbridled logorrhea that spilled out in conversations, at speaking events, and onto volumes of written pages. How could he have gone totally mum on something that would have been such good material? "I doubt the story," Edith says. "But go ahead with it. It can be valuable."

And so I have. The *Kurt Vonnegut, Nazi Slayer!* story conjures up the bloodlust that some of us have for Hollywood stories of good guys beating bad guys. I think it's vital that we be up front about that inclination, one that even Vonnegut himself personally shared. Take a look at the inscription on the next page, which he wrote to a fellow POW, one of eight Americans who banded together after their guards fled.

Edith Vonnegut told me that her father "loved the war," because "it was a great war with a great purpose." He said so himself. After a 1990 talk at the National Air and Space Museum in Washington, DC, Vonnegut was asked if the war had changed his personality. He replied that it had not and that "the war had been a great adventure to me, which I wouldn't have missed for anything."

Vonnegut's response suggests that, for him, war's impact was not simply harrowing, despite that being the foundation for his famous anti-war novel. I point to this contradiction not because it makes me think any less of him or the book but because I think it indicates what a feat he accomplished in writing it. We should not

Courtesy of Vicki Jones Cole.

shy away from inconsistencies. They can be revealing. We need to listen to how people who have experienced war can sometimes surprise us.

When it comes to war, the unexpected abounds. "Every war is ironic because every war is worse than expected," World War II veteran and writer Paul Fussell writes. "Every war constitutes an irony of situation because its means are so melodramatically disproportionate to its presumed ends."

Writer Karl Marlantes, who served in the Marines Corps in Vietnam from 1968 to 1969 and has written several books about war, has compared the experience of his combat with the "exhilaration akin to scoring the winning touchdown."

"You are in a fierce state where there is a primitive and savage joy in doing in your enemy," Marlantes writes in his nonfiction book *What It Is Like to Go to War*. "I used to hesitate to say this, worried it would only further fuel the accusation that we Vietnam veterans were the sick baby killers we were being told we were."

Marlantes tells me that to deny the thrill of war obscures some of its truth. And yet, Tim O'Brien disagrees strongly with what he perceives as the implications of his friend Marlantes's thinking. "I am suspicious of that kind of rhetoric," O'Brien says. "We're going to learn to be better people from killing other people? It's a position where you can justify any war by saying we're going to benefit from it personally and psychologically."

This disagreement points us toward one of the difficult ironies of war and PTSD: that veterans who suffer debilitating effects of trauma sometimes have a hard time overcoming their painful memories because the negative ones are fused with positive ones, such as the camaraderie of living with a band of brothers or the thrill of war that Marlantes speaks of. I think it is Vonnegut's ability to truck in irony that allows him to shine a whole new light on such complexities of war.

It is Vonnegut's dark, sometimes absurd sense of humor that bestows *Slaughterhouse-Five* with an ironic integrity that even an earnest writer such as O'Brien can appreciate. "No one would mistake my prose with Kurt Vonnegut's but we are interested in the same phenomenon," he says. "I'm not interested in bombs and bullets and military maneuvers but I am interested in the twisted labyrinth of memory and its corrosive effect on the human spirit."

In *The Things They Carried*, O'Brien writes, "True war stories do not generalize. They do not indulge in abstraction or analysis. For example: War is hell. As a moral declaration the old truism seems perfectly true, and yet because it abstracts, because it generalizes, I can't believe it with my stomach. Nothing turns inside. It comes down to gut instinct. A true war story, if truly told, makes the stomach believe."

I want to make the case that, by this standard, *Slaughterhouse-Five* is the rare, true war story, one that has been felt in the stomach by countless readers, and that in the decades since its publication, our views of its central themes—war, trauma, and the delicate act of telling war stories—have finally caught up with Vonnegut's accomplishment, allowing us to see it, and the author, more clearly. I believe that, in making this case, it is necessary to explore a particular question that has come to dominate how many readers are today interpreting the book: whether or not *Slaughterhouse-Five* can be used as evidence of its author's undiagnosed PTSD.

This book is a look under the hood of *Slaughterhouse-Five*. I want to trace how Vonnegut was able to write it as if he himself suffered war trauma, even though he said he never did, and why the novel resonates today as a metaphor for PTSD. In the coming chapters, I will present how Vonnegut's life led him to write his "famous Dresden novel," what makes it gut-level true, and why that matters now.

CHAPTER TWO

SLAUGHTERHOUSE-FIVE
AND THE PTSD PRISM

"REREADING *SLAUGHTERHOUSE-FIVE* taught me two things about the novel: how great it really is, and what it's really about. It's not about time travel and flying saucers, it's about PTSD," wrote William Deresiewicz, an author and critic, in *The Nation* magazine in 2012.

Readers have been looking at the book through the psychological trauma prism since the novel first came out. In 1974, literary critic Arnold Edelstein wrote, " 'So it goes' . . . is earned at a price terrible enough to be psychologically consistent with the horror of Billy's experiences. The only way he can live with his memories of his past and his fear of the future and find meaning in both is to withdraw from reality into a pleasant but neurotic fantasy."

In 2019, writer Salman Rushdie gave a talk commemorating the fiftieth anniversary of the novel and said, "It is perfectly possible, perhaps even sensible, to read Billy Pilgrim's entire Tralfamadorian experience as a fantastic, traumatic disorder brought about by his wartime experiences—as 'not real.' Vonnegut leaves that question open, as a good writer should. That openness is the space in which the reader is allowed to make up his or her own mind."

The fiftieth anniversary, which was celebrated with the launch of a special hardcover edition and a series of appreciations in the media, was a moment to reflect on the significance of the book. The *New York Times* framed the novel as "a self-help manual for psychic pain at a time when many young Americans needed it most." Fifty years ago, the Vietnam War was cleaving at the American soul. The plight of the nearly three million veterans who fought it helped define that era. Today, the same number of men and women, 2.7 million, have served in recent conflicts in the Middle East. And with the COVID-19 pandemic killing hundreds of thousands of Americans and upending all our lives, we are going to need as many self-help manuals for psychic pain as we can get.

Approximately 125,000 copies of *Slaughterhouse-Five* were sold in 2019. Across the country people were giving it a first, second, or tenth read. And those sales didn't represent a spike because of the anniversary; throughout the twenty-first century so far, about that same number of copies have been sold every year. It's impossible to track, but those numbers must be dwarfed by the dog-eared, used copies of the book that are lent, borrowed, and stealthily lifted from living room shelves or sold through secondhand bookstores.

I spoke with Steve Almond, bestselling author (*Candyfreak*, *Against Football*), writing professor, and Vonnegut devotee, about why he thinks the book's readership remains strong. But first, a couple notes about Almond: When I say he's a devotee, I should be more clear. Vonnegut is in a league of his own in inspiring years and years of obsessive fans who have read all of his books, quote from them until their friends want to throttle them, and litter their yearbook pages with his wisdom. Almond was once one of those fans. Perhaps you were as well. Almond says he read most of Vonnegut's novels more than six times, in addition to almost everything else he wrote, including his speeches.

Another thing about Almond: I have a distant connection to him and someone I know once pointedly referred to him as a *successful* writer, making me feel about two feet tall. So, I approached him with mixed feelings of awe, envy, and respect. And a wee dram of hostility.

Almond wrote his college thesis on Vonnegut and he almost wrote a biography of him but instead published a seventeen-thousand-word essay titled "Everything Was Beautiful and Nothing Hurt," which he included in his 2007 collection *(Not That You Asked): Rants, Exploits and Obsessions.* In it, Almond astutely writes of Vonnegut: "The evidence was in his books, which performed the greatest feat of alchemy known to man: the conversion of grief into laughter by means of courageous imagination. Like any decent parent, he had made the astonishing sorrow of the examined life bearable."

It's a fantastic piece of writing. Almond explains how Vonnegut inspired him to become a writer and helped him endure his own "family beset with sorrow." So, yes, Almond knows of what he speaks when he tells me that fundamental to *Slaughterhouse-Five*'s appeal is that fans seamlessly identify with both the protagonist and his creator because it feels like nonfiction. "This is what it feels to be me," Almond says of the Vonnegut reader. "This is not just a writer pulling something out of his bag of tricks. He understands me. And it's a byproduct of his traumatic history."

The *Times* article recognized the war trauma of the main character, Billy Pilgrim, which was nothing new. That's been done in countless classrooms, reviews, and dissertation papers. In the book, Pilgrim stumbles between states of catatonia, crying jags, and childlike befuddlement. He also becomes "unstuck in time" and travels to the faraway planet of Tralfamadore, which can be interpreted as actually happening in the narrative or as only occurring in Pilgrim's mind as a symptom of his trauma.

But the Billy-Pilgrim-has-PTSD understanding of the book has more recently budded an interpretation that the trauma of the character also mirrors the author's own. In that *New York Times* article, Kurt's daughter Nanette said her father experienced PTSD and that "he was writing to save his own life . . . and in doing it I think he has saved a lot of lives," meaning that both her father and his readers found healing in *Slaughterhouse-Five*. I imagine reducing his book to a clinical diagnosis or, perhaps worse, putting it in the self-help category, would make Vonnegut shudder.

In a series of conversations, Klinkowitz, who began writing about Vonnegut in the early 1970s, pushed back on my interest in the PTSD connection to *Slaughterhouse-Five*. "When Kurt wants to make a literary character, he is not writing a psychological study," he says. "He is crafting a work of art. In the book he is creating how the world looks to Billy. And it turns out that's how the world looks to most of us. You can learn all you want by talking to psychiatrists but to find out how a character reacts to trauma, you have to create an imaginary construct."

I agree. Vonnegut didn't touch the collective American psyche with a medical text or an anti-war manifesto but with a story spun from his creativity. Although his son, Mark, believes that his father had PTSD and that "you find with combat PTSD that it helps people survive to tell their narrative," he dismisses the notion that his father wrote *Slaughterhouse-Five* with a clear purpose or target. "He was incredibly intuitive. I don't think he had a theory or a strategy," Mark says. "He knew when he had something right but I don't think he could have told you how to get there. And he had no clue what people would think of it."

As it turns out, the book has become what Iraq War veteran Kevin Powers calls a "touchstone" in many peoples' lives, especially that of veterans. Powers, who wrote the foreword to *Slaughterhouse-Five*'s fiftieth anniversary edition, refers to one of his most harrowing war experiences—he was on a rooftop staring through a 4x scope on his M240B machine gun when his fellow soldiers shot and killed an elderly couple who waved a white flag from their car—as his "moment trapped in amber," a moment that remains frozen in his mind, a reference to the Tralfamadorian concept of time and free will.

Powers told me that he drew the jumping-back-and-forth structure of his novel, *The Yellow Birds*, a National Book Award finalist, from *Slaughterhouse-Five*. He relates to being unstuck in time and sees its function in Vonnegut's novel "as this miraculous, perfect device that can represent the trauma response that a lot of veterans have."

"I would argue that this book is among the most humane works of art ever created. It is concerned with and dedicated to the alleviation and prevention of human suffering in the face of its inevitability, and I can think of no braver moral position to take than that one," Powers wrote in his foreword. "You can have Job. I'll throw in my lot with Billy Pilgrim."

Alex Horton, an army infantryman in 2007, carried *Slaughterhouse-Five* to his guard posts in Baghdad and to stations in the Diyala River valley, where he shared it with other soldiers. The book was like a "talisman" for Horton, who could not have then articulated why it was so meaningful to him but later came to realize that the book demonstrated that "this thing that is happening to you right now, these days, will be just as important to you twenty years from now or when you're eighty years old," Horton says. "These things are going to spiral through your life and they are going to attain different meaning as you grow older."

When he got back from Iraq, Horton's feelings of hurt and regret were mitigated by Vonnegut's story, which he turned to for "solace." Horton says that the book was essentially "a blueprint on how to get from Billy Pilgrim to Kurt Vonnegut." And although he didn't specifically try the novelist's path, the Texas-born veteran became a successful *Washington Post* staff writer, covering mostly military matters, committed to the "daily reporting grind."

Without such a blueprint, the imprint of war can often be overwhelming. Many veterans are unable to assimilate their memories of their deployment. Indeed, a lifetime of wrestling with PTSD symptoms has plagued this new generation of soldiers engaged in the "endless wars" of the Middle East. About one in four soldiers has or has had mental health issues. Since the *Diagnostic and Statistical Manual of Mental Disorders* designation of the diagnosis in 1980, there's been increasing awareness and understanding of the ravages of wartime PTSD, a national tragedy that hasn't diminished despite decreased engagements in Iraq and Afghanistan. A total of 6,435 US veterans killed themselves in 2018. And the increase of suicides over the past decade by younger vets, aged eighteen to thirty-five, has been significantly higher than that of non-veterans. It's shocking: Veterans kill themselves at a rate that is two times higher than that of all Americans.

But the legitimacy and growing acceptance of combat PTSD has been tarnished and subsumed by the twin veils of popularization and skepticism. Several factors have contributed to the weakening of the validity of the PTSD diagnosis. It doesn't help that its defining characteristics include that it can be fluid, multifaceted, and lacking in physical properties (although improved brain scans are beginning to reveal more of how PTSD can directly impact neurons).

In the twenty-first century, it feels like anyone can get it. And so, conversely, it seems like no one has it. PTSD has transformed from being a clinical diagnosis to a grab-all description of past pain. I just stepped away from writing these very words and listened to a podcast in which a pundit and a journalist bemoaned their shared "PTSD" from the 2016 election victory of President Trump. The term has become shorthand for anything distressing. When singer Alanis Morissette or actor Keira Knightley claims to have PTSD from the detrimental effects of fame, or actor Shia LaBeouf says he has PTSD from past familial suffering to help explain his bad behavior, however legitimate their pain may be, it dilutes the diagnosis. Furthermore, in a litigious, me-first society, claiming PTSD can translate into financial rewards, which further complicates our understanding of it.

The National Institute of Mental Health ranks PTSD as the third most common mental illness in the United States. In any given year, there are eight million people who suffer from it. Whether or not these numbers are real, inflated, or suppressed almost doesn't matter anymore. This millennium began with the trauma of the September 11 attacks, wars in Afghanistan and Iraq, mass shootings, climate-change-fueled natural disasters, and now COVID-19. Trauma has come to define us as a nation.

Of course, it would be fatuous to suggest our pains are all we are or that they supersede that of previous eras. Without even getting into the genocide of Native Americans and the scourge of slavery, there have always been wars, hard times, and the ravages of disease. But what differs now is that previous generations of the modern era experienced trauma and then, rightly or wrongly, moved on. It was almost like a collective amnesia. Each major war of the twentieth century introduced Americans to the affliction of war trauma anew. Today, PTSD, in its accurate and conflated form, overused or blindly rejected, looks to be settling over us like a permanent haze.

But Vonnegut provided us with a beacon that has time-traveled, unscathed, from the past. The author's two-decade struggle to write a book that depicts the trauma of war truthfully, without cheapening it, anticipated the PTSD diagnosis. "*Slaughterhouse-Five* is the ultimate PTSD novel," says Duke University professor and psychiatrist Harold Kudler, who was the chief consultant for mental health for the US Department of Veterans Affairs (VA) from 2014 to 2018. "It is a fully rendered metaphorical exploration of what it means to be ripped out of your own person, relationships, place and time written by a man who had actually experienced this."

And even more, his story of fractured identity and trips in time and space provides a navigational tool. Billy Pilgrim is a war veteran unlike any other and yet he is universal. Vonnegut circumvented conventions, labels, and false sentiments. He blew all of that up, and by doing so he put a wedge in readers' resistance to ambiguity and complexity. Vonnegut's book, and the way he lived his life, tell us an entirely original story about what it means to be human.

CHAPTER THREE
THE ROAD TO DRESDEN

KURT VONNEGUT may as well have written his own death. He died on April 11, 2007, at the age of eighty-four, after he had tripped on the leash of his small fluffy white dog, Flour, at the bottom of the stairs outside his Manhattan apartment. He suffered head trauma that put him in a coma for weeks. One could not help but think of all the ink he spilled on how much he and his beloved, long-gone sister, Alice, loved a good pratfall or what he once called "people deprived of the dignified postures by gravity." *Bloompity, bloomp, bloomp.*

He had fathered three children, adopted four others, and been married twice. He had published fourteen novels, nine books that could be deemed nonfiction or collections, a bunch of plays and teleplays, one children's book, and scores of short stories and magazine articles, as well as given countless speeches, having been a go-to commencement speaker for decades. His books sold millions of copies. Toward the end of his life, he told his son, Mark, that he was glad to have restored the family fortune that had been lost during the Great Depression.

His success as a writer at the age of forty-six and his ascendency to literary icon status is because of *Slaughterhouse-Five*, which stands at number eighteen—seventeen notches below

Ulysses and one above *Invisible Man*—on the Modern Library's list of the best English-language novels of the twentieth century.

But before we get there, let's trace how his life led to those seminal World War II experiences that eventually begat *Slaughterhouse-Five*.

On November 11, 1922, Vonnegut was born into what his father might have called a family of unicorns, meaning many of them were fortunate enough to live lives steeped in the arts. His ancestors had emigrated from Germany in the middle of the nineteenth century and prospered in Indianapolis, Indiana. Most were well-educated, upper-middle-class merchants.

On his paternal side, Kurt had a great-great-grandfather, Jacob Schramm, who emigrated with five thousand dollars' worth of gold and six hundred books. A great-grandfather, Clemens Vonnegut, came from Westphalia, Germany, in 1848 and started a hardware company that became an Indianapolis mainstay. *Meet you at Vonnegut's* became a common phrase well into the twentieth century.

Kurt identified strongly with Clemens, who was known as a "cultivated eccentric"; he had gotten into some trouble back in Germany when he demonstrated for greater freedoms. In Indiana, he was a rabble-rouser and leader for the cause of improving public education. He was known to feign deafness as a tactic to deflect his critics' arguments. Fond of Benjamin Franklin and Voltaire, Clemens drifted from his Roman Catholic upbringing to become a freethinker, an independent, reason based school of thought that didn't accept dogmas of any kind, particularly religious. He wrote his own "Instruction on Morals," which included the following tenet: "Be aware of this truth that the people on this earth could be joyous, if only they would live rationally and if they would contribute mutually to each other's welfare."

Most of the family history was gathered by a distant relative, John Rauch, known to Kurt as "Uncle John," who wrote a manuscript titled "An Account of the Ancestry of Kurt Vonnegut, Jr., by an Ancient Friend of His Family," and is quoted extensively by Kurt in his *Palm Sunday: An Autobiographical Collage*. Uncle John, who admitted that the record was woefully lacking in details of the female accomplishments in the lineage, sounds like a real wisenheimer. When he read Kurt's 1963 novel, *Cat's Cradle*, he sent him a postcard on which he wrote, "You're saying that life is a load of crap, right? Read Thackeray!"

Both Clemens's son Bernard, and his grandson, Kurt, Kurt Jr.'s father, became architects. Kurt Sr., who drew, painted, and made furniture, said, close to his death in 1957, "It was enough to have been a unicorn."

Freethinking also came from the family of Kurt's mother, Edith. Kurt once said, "I learned my outrageous opinions about religion at my mother's knee." There were great-grandfathers: Peter Lieber, who bought an Indianapolis brewery in 1865 and called it Lieber's Beer, and Karl Barus, a teacher who was a musical steward for the community, a conductor of orchestras, and an organizer of various musical events.

In 1913, Kurt Sr. married Edith, whose family was one of the richest in Indianapolis. The wedding was an opulent, indulgent affair with some six hundred guests, about eighty-five of whom were said to have passed out from too much drinking.

Kurt and Edith lived well and traveled throughout Europe. But the family's fortunes began to turn with the advent of World

War I, when anti-German sentiment cast a pall on their heritage. "The planet they loved and thought they understood was destroyed in the First World War," Kurt once recalled.

It was a grim time for German-Americans. President Woodrow Wilson questioned the loyalty of "hyphenated Americans." German language classes in schools were canceled and even outlawed in places. Even sauerkraut was changed to "liberty cabbage." Das Deutsche Haus, an enormous cultural center and gathering place for Indianapolis's many German immigrants, which Kurt's grandfather Bernard had designed, was vandalized and eventually renamed the Athenæum.

KURT GREW UP in this lengthening shadow in a large brick house that his father had designed in a well-to-do suburb of Indianapolis. Kurt was close to his sister, Alice, who was five years older, and he revered his brother, Bernard, a budding science whiz, who was eight years older than he. Kurt learned to get attention by making his family laugh at his outrageous stories and opinions. Their home was crammed with books. It was also filled with tension between his parents, who had raging arguments.

Although Kurt admitted to absorbing a "bone-deep sadness" from his parents, he recalled his childhood fondly. He had lots of friends and that big, extended family, including a Harvard-educated uncle Alex who pushed him to read socially conscious writers such as John Dos Passos and Eugene Debs.

Vonnegut liked to joke that most of his childhood was spent "building model airplanes and jerking off," but he was also a voracious reader of everything from his uncle Alex's recommendations to pulp fictions, murder mysteries, and science fiction. He also learned he was good at writing. Shortbridge High School, which Kurt's grandfather had designed and his parents had also attended, had its own newspaper and Kurt loved writing articles for an audience of his peers.

The dramatic changes brought by the Depression—Kurt Sr.'s income dropped precipitously—seemed to be felt most by Edith, who had what was then known as schizophrenia but what we would now more likely call manic depression. She would fall into despair and into rages against her husband. Edith treated her condition with barbiturates, a common practice at the time, and she became addicted.

Under the direction of his father and brother, who were intent on him finding a career path as a scientist, Kurt went to Cornell to study chemistry and biology for three years. He spent his spare time working at the *Cornell Daily Sun* newspaper. At the age of twenty, in January 1943, like most men of his generation, he enlisted in the military because it was the right thing to do but also to avoid failing at science at Cornell—the army sent him to Carnegie Mellon and then to the University of Tennessee to study mechanical engineering.

In early 1944, Vonnegut was assigned by the army to train to be a scout at Camp Atterbury in Indiana. It was there that he befriended Bernard V. O'Hare. In May, he got leave to visit his family before heading to fight in Europe. His sister was visiting, too. The night before Mother's Day, Edith took an overdose of barbiturates and died in her sleep. Alice found her the next morning. She and Kurt woke up their father, who was sleeping in another room. Edith did not leave a note and the coroner ruled it an accident, but Kurt later described her death as a suicide.

Private Kurt Vonnegut enlisted in the army in January 1943, when he was twenty years old. Courtesy of the Vonnegut Family Archives.

"She got depressed over what was going on in Germany, the war and everything, and because her son was enlisted in the war," Vonnegut said.

IN OCTOBER, Vonnegut and his division, the 106th, Second Battalion, 423rd Regiment, shipped out on the *Queen Elizabeth* to England to relieve American troops that had been part of the Normandy Invasion. They arrived on the beaches of France by December 6 as part of the final push against Hitler's crumbling army. Ten days later, after riding in trucks and marching through Belgium, they camped in the dense forest of the Ardennes near the Allied front that extended into Germany. It was the 106th's responsibility to hold about a twenty-mile line in the Schnee Eifel region of the forest.

But they arrived just when the Nazis made a last major counteroffensive. German panzer tank divisions shredded the American lines. More than seventy thousand US soldiers were killed, the greatest loss of American life in any single engagement of the war, in what was dubbed the Battle of the Bulge. Vonnegut's 423rd Regiment was cut off from the rest of the division and surrendered on December 19.

Vonnegut wasn't wounded but he was forced to march sixty miles and then stood in a prison freight car for days with little food or water as it slowly transported him and other POWs away from the front. The British Royal Air Force bombed and strafed the train, accidentally killing more than a hundred Allied soldiers. Vonnegut was brought to a prisoner of war camp near Berlin and then later transferred to a work camp in Dresden, where he and his fellow prisoners were held in a slaughterhouse called Schlachthof Fünf.

Dresden was then one of Germany's great cities, having been the capital and royal residence of the illustrious line of Saxon kings for over a hundred years. Settled on both banks of the grand Elbe River, it was, as Vonnegut says in *Slaughterhouse-Five*, known as "Florence on the Elbe," thanks to the prominent baroque and rococo architecture of its museums, opera houses, churches, palaces, and gardens. In addition to being a center of the modern art world, Dresden was known as an industrial and mercantile hub, with banking and car and cigarette factories, among others. It is centrally located between other major cities, including Berlin, to the north and Prague to the south, each about a hundred miles away. During the war, its population had grown from half a million to approximately a million, because refugees flocked to the city, which had been largely left unscathed by combat.

As one of the few Americans who spoke some German, Vonnegut was made a leader of the prisoners. But when he complained about the living conditions to what he later called the "sadistic and fanatical guards" and told them what would happen to them when the Russians overtook the camp, he was beaten and demoted.

On February 13, 1945, eight hundred bombers of the British Royal Air Force rained 1,400 tons of high-explosive bombs over the city, along with more than 1,100 tons of incendiary bombs, which were designed to start fires that ripped through Dresden. Over the next two days, five hundred US planes dropped another thousand tons of explosives on the city's infrastructure, such as railways and bridges. All told, approximately 25,000 civilians were killed, a number far fewer than the 135,000 that Vonnegut wrote of in *Slaughterhouse-Five* (he drew the number from David Irving, a once-respected author whose reputation was destroyed by his anti-Semitism and Holocaust denial), but an atrocity of war nonetheless.

The Allies' stated reasoning for the firebombing was to break up Nazi communication lines to soften defenses as the Russians advanced toward the city, but with the Axis powers crumbling, the more likely motivation was to devastate German morale and as an act of revenge by the British for four years of saturation bombing by the Luftwaffe. Additionally, the city had been functioning as a major rail hub to transport German soldiers. And a portion of its factories—apparently, unbeknownst to Vonnegut— had been retrofitted for its war effort, including the production of optical gun and bomb sights.

In the aftermath, the Nazi guards had the American POWs carry dead Germans to enormous funeral pyres. Surviving civilians would curse and throw rocks at them. But some took pity on them and would surreptitiously bring them food. The prisoners were then transferred to another camp near the Czechoslovakian border, but the guards abandoned it when the German army collapsed in late April.

Vonnegut and seven of his fellow Americans, including Bernard V. O'Hare, spent the next eight days scavenging after returning to Dresden. They commandeered a horse-drawn wagon and filled it up with loot. They drank with German soldier stragglers who, fearing the Russians far more than the Americans, tried to ingratiate themselves.

In letters to his family, the young Vonnegut wrestled with describing the horrors he'd seen. He tried brightening the mood. In one letter that they didn't actually receive, he wrote, "It is a source of great delight to be able to announce that you will shortly receive a splendid relic of World War II with which you may decorate your hearth—namely, me in an excellent state of preservation. You may well say 'Huzzah!' for this prodigal princeling has survived."

On May 29, Kurt successfully sent his father another letter telling him that he wasn't "missing in action," as Kurt Sr. had been informed by the army—it must have been an excruciating six months for the Vonnegut family—and that he was in a repatriation camp in Le Havre, getting ready to come back to the States. A month later, Kurt was driving his father's Dodge up the Indiana freeway from Camp Atterbury to his family home in Indianapolis. In the car with him were his father, his sister, and his uncle Alex. Kurt had lost more than forty pounds and was talking a mile a minute. He wanted to know what news of the Dresden bombing had reached the US. He spoke of how a fellow soldier had died of starvation and that giving up mentally had led to his demise. He also told them about the execution of an American "boy" for stealing string beans.

"The sons of bitches! The sons of bitches!" he cried, looking ahead at the road through tears.

CHAPTER FOUR
ONWARDS AND UPWARDS

IN THE SUMMER OF 1945, Vonnegut wanted to leave the war behind him. Stationed in Kansas as a clerk-typist, he was full of poetic visions of his future. He was eager to exit the army, start a family, and hopefully launch a writing career. Happily, he had the perfect partner: Jane Cox, a fair, bookish girl, a foot shorter than he, whom he'd known since kindergarten, and with whom he'd rekindled a relationship during their college years while he was at Cornell and she was at Swarthmore.

By August, they were planning a mutual life together. "You scare me when you say that I am going to create the literature of 1945 onwards and upwards," he wrote to her in a letter. "Angel, will you stick by me if it goes backwards and downwards?" In Kansas, Vonnegut wrote short stories and sent them to Jane, who would edit them.

Despite there being concerns about their respective family histories of mental illness (Jane's mother "went insane periodically," according to Kurt), they married in September 1945. Both were writers; in fact, Vonnegut claimed in a letter that he thought she was the better one of the two of them. She was certainly a better reader; she recommended books to him, including

Dostoevsky's *The Brothers Karamazov*, which he took with him during their honeymoon.

They both shared conventional ideas about the roles of a husband and wife, and so their plan was for him to become the professional writer to support their family—they hoped to have seven children—in a life steeped in a vibrant exchange of ideas with a group of cultured friends.

"These were incredibly romantic people who believed in the arts," Nanette says. "What my mother and father stressed was that the arts were not an extracurricular activity; it was fundamental to them. It was how you become more human."

Vonnegut plotted an early career path that would allow him to write books. He considered teaching, journalism, or getting a job as an advertising copywriter. "You've given me the courage to decide to be a writer," he wrote to Jane. "That much of my life has been decided. Regardless of my epitaph, to be a writer will have been my personal ultimate goal."

Jane had rapt faith in her husband's potential. As relayed in Charles Shields's biography of Vonnegut, *And So It Goes*, she submitted several of his stories to a writing consultant, author Scammon Lockwood, and told him that she considered her husband "a potential Chekhov." Although he was mildly encouraging, Lockwood politely advised that Vonnegut should lower his sights from "uplift[ing] humanity" and instead write "current literature," meaning popular, and more potentially remunerative, storytelling.

When the newlyweds were both accepted for graduate studies at the University of Chicago—a track toward teaching—they moved to an apartment with a view of Lake Michigan. Vonnegut abandoned the fields of science that his brother and father had hoped for him and instead entered the Anthropology Department, which he found to be an "intellectual kick."

Vonnegut immersed himself in how human cultures functioned and evolved at a time when civilization had come back from the brink. The world was starting anew, just like the young couple. As a passionate romantic, Vonnegut's ideals extended into fervent political views. He shows his moxie—to the point that it suggests he's half-kidding—in a letter he wrote to his brother, Bernard, and his sister-in-law, Bow, on Memorial Day of 1946, encouraging them to advocate for a "real world federation," decrying the incipient United Nations as an "enfeebled fiasco."

The typed letter starts with a handwritten "Huzzah!" He then implores them to write to President Harry Truman for the cause. "The decision is for our generation to make. If we make the wrong one, you, Bow, and you, Bernard, and your son, will be killed deader than hell. There will be nothing left. If you don't try to do something, if you don't believe what I have said is true—then you are either incredibly stupid or crazy as bed bugs."

He says that he fears an atomic Holocaust, reminding his brother and sister-in-law, "I'll not forget Dresden," before signing off, "Love (that ceases to be when humanity ceases to be)."

At the time, Vonnegut's passion impressed an older cousin, Walt, who was also attending the University of Chicago. Cousin Walt wrote that Kurt displayed a remarkably "eager intelligence."

But the passion and smarts didn't necessarily mean he was a good fit in the strictures of the Anthropology Department. His thesis, which paralleled Cubist painters and the artistry of Plains Indians, was rejected after more than two years of study. He was already working part-time as a newspaper reporter and he didn't see the point of continuing with school. Vonnegut began looking for a full-time job outside of academia. Jane had already dropped out after becoming pregnant with their first child, Mark, who was born on May 11, 1947.

Vonnegut sent out a letter to potential employers to help explain his uneven academic career, which included no degree from either Cornell or the University of Chicago. "I took [anthropology] up as part of a personal readjustment following some bewildering experiences as an infantryman and later as a prisoner of war in Dresden, Germany," he wrote.

All the while, Vonnegut was writing short stories, with edits from Jane. Some of the stories were inspired by his war experiences, such as "Brighten Up!" and "Atrocity Story," the former a banal, dark tale about a loan shark at an American POW camp and the latter about a similar camp where a prisoner is executed by the Nazis. All of his stories were rejected by magazine editors.

In late 1947, Vonnegut had job offers at a publishing house and a newspaper, but he and Jane opted instead to move to the town of Alplaus in upstate New York to be near his brother who worked as a research scientist at General Electric, where he helped Kurt get a job in the public relations department.

Not one to be boxed in, Kurt quickly grew to hate the drudgery of being a pitchman for GE, although he found good source material for his writing. Finally, in February of 1950, he had his first short story published. "Report on the Barnhouse Effect," a sci-fi tale about a man with the telekinetic powers to "flatten anything on earth," was printed in *Collier's* magazine, which was championing the short story genre.

Vonnegut was paid $750 for the story, which was equal to two months of his GE salary. He wrote a letter to his father, crowing, "I think I'm on my way." He planned to get four more published and then quit his job and never work another "nightmare job" again.

Vonnegut resigned at the end of the year so that he could write full-time, something even his *Collier's* editor, Knox Burger, considered a precarious decision. But after selling three stories to Burger, Vonnegut and Jane had enough money to rent a summer house in Cape Cod, where Vonnegut ran into writer Norman Mailer, also a World War II veteran, whose "great war novel," as Vonnegut called it at the time, 1948's *The Naked and the Dead*, had been a bestseller. Mailer, who was a few months younger than Vonnegut, was the very model of success that he aspired to be.

The Vonneguts had Mailer over at their house for a drink at a time when Vonnegut could finally call himself a full-fledged writer, "not red hot, but self-supporting," he would later say. But he could only dream of gaining the acceptance that Mailer had achieved. The air must have been thick with competition: Vonnegut later told Mailer that after the more successful writer left the house, Vonnegut's mother-in-law, many drinks in, said loudly, "Well—I think you're cuter than he is" to her son-in-law.

The Vonneguts were enamored with Cape Cod and decided to move there permanently, near the airport that Kurt bullishly anticipated would help him facilitate frequent trips to New York City to meet with editors. By leaving Alplaus, Vonnegut may have moved physically farther away from the big city, but he was making his way closer to New York's insular literary world.

Although his short story success remained limited, he turned a corner when Charles Scribner's, the prestigious publisher, put out his first novel, *Player Piano*, in August 1952. The book tells of a dystopian world in which automation has reoriented society into grim casts. The lead character rebels against the mechanization and groupthink. Yes, as Vonnegut would later admit, he "cheerfully ripped off the plot of *Brave New World*," by Aldous Huxley.

One could see how the book was heavily influenced by Vonnegut's experiences working at General Electric, where he had witnessed industrial innovations in engineering and technology that pointed to an emphasis on efficiency and conformity. He appropriated his nonfiction reality for fiction, even using a few actual names, such as mathematician John von Neumann, for characters.

The book wasn't a hit, not quite selling half of its original 7,600 print run, and it received a smattering of reviews. But it did get some acclaim from fans of science fiction. It was successful enough that Scribner's signed up Vonnegut for another book.

But any accomplishments were tempered by constant rejections from editors. Vonnegut felt like an outsider who couldn't break through. He swore off going to New York, bemoaning how the bar around the corner from Scribner's, where writers and editors congregated, "always makes me feel like the dullest bastard on earth."

Vonnegut would often call himself a "hack," a writer who'd do anything for money. He would work in the mornings for several hours and then go for walks with his dog. He was churning out stories, which Jane would send out to editors. And then she would compile an ever-expanding file of rejection slips.

But it was worse when he was unable to write, which would happen occasionally. In 1953, he asked his editor, and now friend, Knox Burger, if he could help him find a psychotherapist. "The nut of the matter is that I can't write anymore, and I'm not very nice to my family anymore either," he wrote. Vonnegut was worried about how "things are getting somewhat sticky with me mentally" and that he'd become "unenthusiastic." Within a couple years, he'd say he felt the same as his sister, Alice, who also struggled financially, agreeing that they were "well fed-up with the character-building aspects of disappointment."

But Vonnegut endeavored to find ways to think through his problems. He and Jane ran a Great Books Course in Cape Cod; that inspired him to begin to write plays for theater, which he found enervating. "The philosophical restrictions of slick short stories finally whipped me. The formal restrictions of plays are delightful and stimulating," he wrote in a letter to his Scribner's editor and friend Harry Brague.

For uplift, Vonnegut and Jane spent a two-day vacation surreptitiously sitting in on classes at Harvard. "More fun than a barrel of monkeys, till reeled the mind," he said of listening to professors Arthur Schlesinger Sr. on the Hudson River School of painting, Arthur Schlesinger Jr. on American literature, and Pitirim Sorokin on historian Oswald Spengler.

In 1954, Vonnegut was having more success selling short stories to publications such as *Esquire*, *Cosmopolitan*, and the *Saturday Evening Post*. He sold seven stories that year. The Vonneguts bought a bigger house in Barnstable, also on the Cape, for their expanding family; daughters Edith and Nanette were born in 1949 and 1954, respectively. But any success was subsumed by the overwhelming pressure of feeling like a writing failure. Nanette recalls the family lore that the day she was born her father was sobbing at the hospital, after almost driving off a bridge on the way over.

Vonnegut hustled for work, such as a stint writing copy for *Sports Illustrated*. But he didn't have the temperament for it. He

Kurt and Jane with their children, Mark, Edith, and Nanette in 1955,
three years before they would adopt the Adams boys.
Courtesy of the Vonnegut Family Archives.

walked away from the job after being given the assignment to write a caption for a photo of a horse jumping over a fence. He wrote, "The horse jumped over the fucking fence," and left his desk, never to return.

Over a five-year period, Vonnegut scrambled to find ways to supplement his writing income. He proposed a gimmick bow tie to a friend who owned a shirt-making company. He pitched a war strategy game that could be played on a checkerboard with pieces representing "artillery, infantry, armored, and airborne units" to an Ohio game company. He also worked for an industrial advertising agency in Boston and taught English at a private school "for seriously fucked-up rich kids," as he wrote later. At least he was paid a hefty sum of a thousand dollars to build an eighteen-foot sculpture for a restaurant at Boston's Logan Airport.

In 1957, Kurt's father, Kurt Sr., died after a bout with lung cancer, leaving his children an inheritance he'd accumulated from investments in the stock market. But Kurt Jr. poured the money into a pipe dream; after driving behind a truck loaded with Saab cars, he came up with a scheme to open his own Saab dealership because he was convinced his Cape Cod neighbors would be wowed by European flair and Swedish engineering. But it was a bust: After buying six cars out of pocket to be resold, he shut down the failed business within less than a year.

His father's passing put Kurt Jr. in a creativity spiral. He struggled to write the second book for Scribner's and worked on a third novel in fits and starts. And then, just a year after his father's death, his sister, Alice, began to succumb to cancer herself. On September 15, 1958, she was on her deathbed at the hospital when her husband, Jim Adams, took a New Jersey commuter train from their home to a business meeting. But the train's engineer had a heart attack, causing the train to derail into a river, killing forty-nine people, including Adams. Alice died thirty-six hours later.

The shock and tragedy of his sister's and brother-in-law's deaths had a profound effect on Vonnegut, far more than the war, according to the author, who was so close to Alice that he considered her his first muse, the audience of one that he wrote all of his books for.

Kurt and Jane adopted three of the Adams boys, who ranged in age from eight to fourteen; a fourth, who was two years old, ended up with other relatives. Kurt was left to contend with a cataclysmic circumstance seemingly beyond imagining and a whole new set of responsibilities. Trying to explain how he handled his sister's death, Kurt's daughter Nanette tells a favorite story of her father's: A woman loses control of her car and drives it through an entire suburban neighborhood, plowing through gates, mail-boxes, and shrubbery. When she finally comes to a halt, she is asked why she didn't take her foot off the gas. "I was too busy steering," she replies.

The train crash was big enough news and the circum-stances of the Vonneguts so tragic that they were featured in several newspapers, including the *New York Post*, which sent a reporter who wrote a story about the misfortunes of the young family and described Vonnegut's eyes as "red rimmed with grief and fatigue and his voice trembles." The Vonneguts were in crisis mode. While Jane ran the household, Kurt was under even more pressure to craft stories that would sell. He smoked constantly as he craned his six-foot-two-inch frame over his typewriter, which was placed on a low table.

In 1959, after being denied a Guggenheim Fellowship, he asked Burger in a letter, "When one is being frog-marched by life, does one giggle or does one try to maintain as much dignity as possible under the circumstances?"

Vonnegut's second book, *The Sirens of Titan*, was pub-lished that year. Set in the twenty-second century, *Titan* is about the richest man in America, who is able to travel through gaps in the space-time continuum to different planets. More than *Player Piano*, *Titan* is squarely a science fiction novel, replete with armies from Mars and a robot from a distant planet named Tralfamadore.

The Sirens of Titan had a small first print run, and although it was nominated for the Hugo Award, a literary award for sci-ence fiction, for best novel, it didn't sell well. Despite its lack of commercial success, Vonnegut was entering a prolific phase of his career, churning out short stories for the *Saturday Evening*

Post, Redbook, Ladies' Home Journal, and others. The stories for the "slicks" were part of Vonnegut's pipeline to finance his family of eight while he also worked on his novels. His brother-in-law's family also provided monetary support but it never seemed to be enough.

Vonnegut worked in a ground-floor room, which was set off from the rest of the house by a series of doors where he wrote in the morning. He liked to say that a person is only smart for three hours of the day. After writing in the morning, he would go for walks along the beach with his dog, Sandy. Later, Jane would make him a sweet Rob Roy, a Scotch whiskey drink with vermouth and bitters, and he'd work some more while Jane read his latest story or chapter in the adjoining study. If she laughed out loud, he'd perk up and come out to see what she was responding to. He would also sometimes get angry after drinking, not getting fall-down drunk, but occasionally there would be loud rows with Jane.

Vonnegut's discipline as a writer could be heard and smelled in the house. There was the constant sound of his Smith-Corona clanking away. And the strong bouquet of coffee and Pall Malls permeated his quarters. With so many kids running around, he seemed to be in a world removed. "Working his ass off, sitting still," Nanette says.

And the kids didn't know what they'd get when he'd come out of his room. Sometimes, there was elation. But mostly, not. "It didn't look like much fun what my father was going through," Nanette says.

He could be moody. The blended families of the Vonneguts and the Adams kids in a ramshackle house with a large outdoor space was a draw for many of the neighborhood kids, who would come to play games like daring each other to do gross things. When they got raucous, Vonnegut would come out and yell at the kids to "shut the hell up!"

Although he scared them, Vonnegut could also be playfully eccentric, instigating games such as catching the abundant flies around the house or going on swimming trips or treks through the marsh. His sense of fun could also sometimes be a bit cruel. He would pit his children against each other, making a game of who was the better artist. "It was a joke but it wasn't," Nanette says.

"We were a really big, crazy, sloppy, happy family and we didn't have a lot of fame or anything. Just a lot of kids running around," Edith says. In addition to children, there were words everywhere. Vonnegut picked up a proclivity from his father to put up phrases that had meaning to him. He scrawled, "God damn it, you have to be kind" (Mark said his father put greater emphasis on the first three words), "Go, love without the help of anything on earth" (from poet William Blake), and "Ye shall love one another" (the New Testament) on the walls or carved them into furniture. Near the phone, people wrote important phone numbers on the wall. Of course, there were also the stacks and stacks of typed pages with coffee stains strewn about the house, which was also filled with books.

The house was a mess, but not for Jane's lack of trying. And she issued written directives of her own, posting notes around the house, such as "Flush the toilet" and "Put dirty clothes in the hamper," on which others would scribble wiseass retorts.

According to Nanette, her father communicated best with the written word. "What he did in writing was very loving," she recalls. His way of loving people was in his letters. "In person, he had a hard time being consistently connected and warm. But he was of the generation of fathers who weren't affectionate. And my mother made up for it."

In addition to 1961's *Canary in a Cat House*, an anthology of his short stories, his third novel, *Mother Night*, came out as a 35-cent paperback original. The novel is told in the first person by Howard Campbell, an American spy who functions as a propagandist for Nazi Germany. The not especially likable Campbell narrates the story from a prison cell while on trial in Nuremberg. He may be a victim of circumstance but he's a ripe subject to plumb the ambiguity of one's actions during war. The story's moral is plainly summed up by Vonnegut, who later added an introduction in which he wrote, "We are what we pretend to be, so we must be careful about what we pretend to be."

The book was hardly noticed and went unreviewed by major reviewers. Two years later, in 1963, *Cat's Cradle* came out. Vonnegut had been working on the book for over a decade, having gleaned its primary theme when he was working at GE. He had heard a story that H. G. Wells had visited the company's science labs and was given a tour by its lead scientist, Irving Langmuir, who suggested the author could write a book about a form of ice that doesn't melt at room temperature. And when it solidifies all of the water on the planet, Armageddon ensues.

Wells didn't take up the idea but it stuck with Vonnegut, who wrote of "ice-nine," a substance that makes water freeze instantaneously and is weaponized with the potential to destroy the planet, the plot driver in a madcap atomic-age allegory.

The book, which is spread out over 127 chapters, some less than a page long, opening and closing like a blinking eye— Vonnegut later said he structured each chapter as if it were a joke—was a hit with college kids hungry for narratives that questioned the status quo with an irreverent tone, such as 1961's *Catch-22*, by Joseph Heller. Soon, they would be flocking to theaters to see Stanley Kubrick's 1964 Cold War parody, *Dr. Strangelove or: How I Learned to Stop Worrying and Love the Bomb*. In *Cat's Cradle*, Vonnegut juxtaposes a ludicrous religious leader, Bokonon, who pushes a benevolent creed of "shameless lies," with an Oppenheimer-like scientist, who invents "ice-nine" without any concern for its application.

Despite its underground following and a laudatory review in the *New York Times* by novelist Terry Southern ("an irreverent and often highly entertaining fantasy," he wrote), *Cat's Cradle* didn't get much more attention from the literary establishment than *Mother Night* did, and the book didn't sell through its initial 6,000 print run.

Jane did what she could to move books, though. She would go into local bookstores and use a false name to order her husband's books so that the store would have them in stock.

It took Vonnegut just a year to complete his next novel, *God Bless You, Mr. Rosewater, or Pearls Before Swine*, which was published in 1965. In the book, the lead character, Eliot Rosewater, is a disturbed millionaire who has been traumatized by his World War II experience of killing three German firefighters whom he mistook for Nazi soldiers. As a super-wealthy son of a senator, Rosewater is at risk of losing his inheritance if he is proven to be insane. But in a book that practically screams that it has something important to say, Rosewater's sanity is really a stand-in for a larger question: Is the whole American class system what's nuts?

Rosewater garnered Vonnegut the best reviews of his career, and it was his first book to sell through its first print run. The *New*

York Times reviewer, although noting a perplexing, "unique narrative style" that came across as "random meditations," still complimented Vonnegut for "an excellent ear, a knack for arresting imagery, and a Message." Not that it received universal acclaim: the *New Yorker* review condemned the book as "a series of narcissistic giggles."

CHAPTER FIVE
WRITING *SLAUGHTERHOUSE-FIVE*, OR, THIS LOUSY LITTLE BOOK

"I WOULD HATE TO TELL YOU what this lousy little book cost me in money and anxiety and time," Vonnegut writes in the opening chapter of *Slaughterhouse-Five*. "When I got home from the Second World War twenty-three years ago, I thought it would be easy for me to write about the destruction of Dresden, since all I would have to do would be to report what I had seen."

It is impossible to record exactly how and when Vonnegut wrote *Slaughterhouse-Five*, because for most of those twenty-three years he was working on the book concurrently with his other writing. And he wrote material for his other books, short stories, and essays that end up in *Slaughterhouse-Five*. Vonnegut alternated between explicitly and implicitly writing *Slaughterhouse-Five* as a sort of shadow novel that looms over all of his writing.

"You see it in the early works; you see him taking up pieces of it," says State University of New York at Fredonia professor Christina Jarvis, another Vonnegut scholar. (She has a goldfish named Kilgore Trout.) "I defy you to find a novel that doesn't have a veteran character in it. Even when he is not writing about war, he is writing about war. *Slaughterhouse-Five* was hanging over him."

You can almost see the outline of the novel in Vonnegut's May 29, 1945, letter to his family informing them for the first time of his survival as a POW. It is mostly a report of what he had seen, including the deaths of two fellow POWs who end up being foundational for the novel, and it also displays the grim wit and signature style that would define Vonnegut's later writing. He sardonically refers to his captors as "the supermen" and implements a refrain after mentioning the horrifying deaths of others. First, he uses "But I didn't," after describing Americans who died during the march after being captured, and then, twice, he writes "But not me," after describing the Germans who were killed in Dresden and then fellow POWs who were accidentally killed by Russians.

The letter hints at the darkly ironic yet profoundly life-affirming view of a young soldier who has been through hell. It's a tone he struggled with. A week earlier, he wrote in another letter, "This letter started as a huge joke. There's no sense in going through with it. There's nothing funny in watching friends starve to death or in carrying body after body out of inadequate air-raid shelters to mass kerosene funeral pyres—and that is what I've done these past six months."

At twenty-two years old, as Vonnegut wrestled with how to relay his story to his family back home, he was also developing a literary voice. Fellow Slaughterhouse Five POW Tom Jones said, "As far back as sitting on the boat over from Europe, Vonnegut began working on turning his war experiences into a narrative."

After returning to Indianapolis, in November 1945, Vonnegut read an article in *Newsweek* about the war and was struck by how valuable his experience had been: "Everything that was reported by ace newsmen from the heart of Europe I found to be old stuff to me," he wrote in a letter. "By Jesus, I was there."

Vonnegut's initial impulse was to emulate other veterans who wrote "classy" adventures about the war, such as eventual *60 Minutes* opinion writer Andy Rooney, who published *Air Gunner*, with co-author Bud Hutton, in 1944. The book is a series of hard-boiled accounts of the young men who face death daily as they blast Nazis with their aerial machine guns. But Vonnegut's earliest recorded attempts to write a war story were sophomoric and didactic. In a 1946 or 1947 essay titled "Wailing Shall Be in All Streets," he writes of being "sick at heart" by the massacre he had witnessed. "I was there," he pleadingly writes. In another nonfiction piece, "I Shall Not Want," he writes of what it felt like to starve as a POW. These and other pieces were not accepted by editors for publication until after Vonnegut became famous.

But he kept at it. Excited by the prospects of the new television medium, the young Vonnegut also wrote of Dresden in a teleplay format that appears to have undergone several title changes, including "I'll Go to Sleep in Dresden," "A Dresden Goodnight," and "Slaughterhouse-Five." Professor Jarvis estimates that Vonnegut wrote the teleplays between 1954 and 1957. In one of these versions, two Jewish-American soldiers have survived the Dresden bombing but they are locked in a slaughterhouse, where they fear they will languish and die unless their young Nazi guard lets them out. In another version, there are two POWs and one of them survives the war and becomes a playwright who writes a play within the teleplay in order to reveal how his fellow soldier was killed. "He has chosen to tell the deeply disturbing truth by means of a play, since only through art can he hope to recreate the atmosphere in which the murder took place," Vonnegut writes in a treatment.

In 1964 or 1965, Vonnegut's writing of *Slaughterhouse-Five* turned a critical corner. He took his daughter, Nanette, and her friend Allison Mitchell on a trip from their home in Barnstable to see the World's Fair in New York City, with a side visit to Bernard V. O'Hare in Pennsylvania. Vonnegut had been working in fits and starts on the war book, and he hoped a sit-down with his old war buddy would refresh some memories and thoughts that had eluded him so far.

Vonnegut's rendition of the trip has been immortalized in the first chapter of *Slaughterhouse-Five*.

He describes the moment as an important departure in his thinking when he realized he had to expose war for what it is: a tragic tale of children being asked to kill other children. But what doesn't appear on the page is how the trip to Pennsylvania also inspired a fundamental shift in the structure of the novel.

Professor Jarvis, who has spent much more time than I at the Lilly Library, has steeped herself in Vonnegut (she peppers her emails with Vonnegutisms, including sign-offs such as "Until the accident wills" and "From Gehard Müller's taxi cab"), and for the past six years has been working on papers and seminars and a book. Along the way, she unearthed a March 23, 1965, letter from Sam Stewart, Vonnegut's friend and early book editor, that indicates the author was developing the framing of the novel around the Pennsylvania trip way back then. When he went there to dig up stories of World War II, he came back with the idea of turning the trip itself into the foundation of a meta-narrative novel.

"I cannot help but hope that you find it possible to frame it in the present," Stewart writes of Vonnegut's experience visiting

Bernard V. O'Hare. "It seems to me a perfect vehicle for the telling. And it would make it a very different book."

Stewart was responding to an earlier letter or conversation between the men. "I don't mean to suggest how you should write it: I'm only going by what you told me and what impressed me," he adds.

In *Slaughterhouse-Five*, Vonnegut writes that the trip happened "in 1964 or so—whatever the last year was for the New York World's Fair," and although the fair occurred in 1964 and 1965, it's more likely this actually happened in its first year, considering Stewart's letter to Vonnegut reflecting back on it in early 1965, before the fair began again in April.

"THE MAJOR COMPOSITIONAL PERIOD was between 1965 and 1968," Jarvis says. Indeed, over those four years, Vonnegut worked his way closer toward the subject in actual *Slaughterhouse* drafts and in his other writing. He had already written war trauma into *Rosewater* with the title character, who was troubled by his World War II experience of killing the three Germans, having a vision of Indianapolis engulfed in a firestorm like the one he reads about in a book about Dresden.

At the same time that he was inching toward including the content of his Dresden experiences in his novels, Vonnegut was increasingly experimenting with the metafictional form, incorporating his nonfiction reality into his fiction. In a draft version of *Cat's Cradle*, he put the name "Vonnegut" on a gravestone of a relative of the narrator, but was dissuaded by his editor because it was too genre-bending. Instead, he settled for referring to an unspecified "screwy" German name.

This evolution of his craft and subject matter was tied to the vicissitudes of the short story market, which began to decline thanks largely to the shift in advertising dollars toward television. Publications such as the *Saturday Evening Post* began to tighten their budgets and *Collier's* completely folded in 1957. Vonnegut began to write more nonfiction. He wrote essays and reviews for publications such as the *New York Times Book Review, McCall's*, and *Life*, as a new nonfiction movement, later to be dubbed New Journalism by Tom Wolfe in 1973, was emerging. Writers such as Southern, Joan Didion, Gay Talese, and Hunter S. Thompson were loosening the traditional strictures of nonfiction journalism with evocative and first-person techniques. Truman Capote's *In Cold Blood*, a nonfiction tale about a Kansas murder spree that read breathtakingly like fiction, first excerpted in the *New Yorker* in 1965, was the leading light in the genre.

Vonnegut began playing with New Journalism techniques. He wrote essays as if they were fiction, such as 1964's short story "Where I Live," which includes the point of view of what might be a made-up encyclopedia salesman in an otherwise actual, socio-historical survey of Vonnegut's adopted hometown of Barnstable. He would later say that he would "guess" that he was a New Journalist.

He was a big fan of Thompson's writing. He also began putting himself at the center of his nonfiction stories, such as 1966's "Brief Encounters on the Inland Waterway," about riding the Kennedy family yacht from Massachusetts to Florida. (No Kennedys were on the boat at the time.)

Writing about cruising on the family boat of his illustrious Cape Cod neighbors placed Vonnegut in a role he felt in his bones: the consummate outsider, finding his own skewed way to look in. Just the year before, his seventeen-year-old daughter, Edith, had performed in a local theater production of *Treasure Island* after which eight-year-old Caroline Kennedy, the daughter of recently assassinated president John F. Kennedy, approached her, "wide-eyed," according to Vonnegut, on the lawn outside the theater and asked her for her autograph.

Vonnegut both embraced and chafed at his outsider's status. "I have been a soreheaded occupant of a file drawer labeled 'science fiction,'" he wrote in 1965's *Wampeters, Foma and Granfalloons*. "And I would like out, particularly since so many serious critics regularly mistake the drawer for a urinal."

In Barnstable, he felt far from New York's literary center, surrounded by all those "damn kids" and neighbors who didn't read his work, let alone writers with whom he could commiserate. Although, it's true, he did meet one sort-of literary luminary who moved to Cape Cod in the late fifties: Theodore Sturgeon, a renowned science fiction writer whose many novels and stories included *Killdozer!* and "Granny Won't Knit." The Vonneguts hosted a dinner for Sturgeon and his wife in Barnstable. Sturgeon inspired Vonnegut's oft-used fictional character, Kilgore Trout, a lugubrious failure of a science fiction writer who serves as a stand-in for Vonnegut in many of his novels, including *Slaughterhouse-Five*.

But for Vonnegut, Sturgeon was a cautionary tale of what he might become—hardly the sort of fellow traveler who could pierce the loneliness of being on the Cape. He supplanted this isolation by writing copious letters to his peers, especially Knox Burger, whom he implored to come up to visit him to go on fishing trips.

His writing was his most constant companion. He would hunch over his typewriter and write and rewrite the same page over and over again, muttering to himself, lighting another cigarette, reading his words out loud, and then pulling the paper out of the typewriter and ripping it up to start over again. "Writing was a spiritual exercise for my father, the only thing he really believed in," wrote Mark, who also told me, "Without writing, he could have been just another drunk, homeless, or addicted vet who died on the street."

Finally, a way out of his Cape Cod confinement appeared in the spring of 1964; poet Robert Lowell dropped out of teaching at the prestigious Iowa university creative writing program, and Vonnegut was offered the position, which he took, eager for the money, to be in a community of fellow writer-teachers and to be away from his family. He also hoped that it would be a good setting to work on his Dresden book.

Vonnegut went to Iowa in Mark's car jammed with books and many drafts of his unfinished war novel. He was a writer with a flailing career and no more than a high school degree, eager to make an impression; Vonnegut read Flaubert's *Madame Bovary* and recent works by Louis-Ferdinand Céline and Theodore Roethke. He believed he would be seen as an amateur, a sci-fi scribbler compared to the other writing workshop professionals, who included National Book Award winner Nelson Algren, Fulbright poet Charles Wright, and William Faulkner Foundation Prize winner José Donoso.

He hoped his sense of humor would catch on with the students. Initially, though, his classes were uneven at best. His irreverent attitude toward the literary establishment alienated some of the budding writers. They didn't know what to make of the tall teacher who wrote "Fuck" on the chalkboard on his first day of teaching and pronounced, "If the magazine you want to write for doesn't embrace this word, don't use it."

Some of his students, who were seeking Masters in Fine Arts degrees, were promising, such as aspiring writer John Irving (later bestselling novelist of *The World According to Garp*, etc.). In class, Vonnegut read his own short story, "Harrison Bergeron," which had been published in the *Magazine of Fantasy and Science Fiction* in 1961, out loud. The dystopian story takes place in America in the year 2081, when citizens are handicapped so that everyone has equal abilities and opportunities in a thinly veiled critique of the socialism of the USSR. By one student's estimate, a third of the students loved it, but most were skeptical.

Vonnegut focused his teaching on how his students could sell their work and how they should write for an audience, including a lesson in which he adapted his rejected University of Chicago thesis paper, "Fluctuations Between Good and Ill Fortune in Simple Tales." In the lesson, he half-seriously reduced storytelling to ups and downs on graph charts that he could draw on the blackboard.

It was challenging for Vonnegut, but he savored the change of pace. Separated from his family, Vonnegut's eye began to wander. According to biographer Charles Shields, he had had other dalliances with women, but at Iowa he had his most serious affair, with one of his students, Loree Wilson, an attractive divorced mother of two, who was in her thirties. He told her that he was "estranged" from his wife, and they began what he later referred to in *Slaughterhouse-Five* as "some perfectly beautiful trouble." Despite the relationship, Vonnegut hosted a visit from Jane. And their daughter Edith even lived with him for a semester of high school. He was able to maintain the subterfuge but his marriage was coming apart.

Without either an undergraduate or graduate degree, Vonnegut was at the bottom of the pay scale at Iowa, so he continued to write reviews and essays for different publications, including an October 1966 review of the new edition of the Random House dictionary for the *New York Times*. The review, which appeared during his second year at Iowa, is incisive (he deduces that the word *prescriptive* is "like an honest cop," in contrast to *descriptive*, which he likens to "a boozed-up war buddy from Mobile, Ala") and anything but boring (he looks up *hump* and recalls his childhood of looking up dirty words).

The review caught the eye of editor Seymour Lawrence, who had an imprint at Dell. Lawrence was in the business of grooming writers. The two men met and Lawrence offered Vonnegut a three-book deal for $75,000, the first of which would be his novel-in-progress, *Slaughterhouse-Five*. It was a huge sum for Vonnegut, who told Lawrence, "That's too much money—you'll never get it back."

Lawrence replied, "You worry about writing, I'll worry about money."

In 1967, his new editor began consolidating Vonnegut's backlog of writing with reprints and a new volume of his short stories and essays, 1968's *Welcome to the Monkey House*, which became Lawrence's first Vonnegut book. Never mind that the *New York Times* review called it "old soup" and that "this book says much against 'collections'"; it was a deliberate attempt by Lawrence to prime the industry, from reviewers to booksellers, for his author's upcoming novel. Vonnegut's work was also, for the first time, the subject of serious academic appraisal when University of Iowa English professor Robert Scholes grouped him with a cadre of innovative writers, including Southern, John Barth, Iris Murdoch, and John Hawkes, in his book *The Fabulators*.

Vonnegut was increasingly being discussed in literary circles as part of an emerging so-called Black Humorist movement—better-known names were Joseph Heller, Thomas Pynchon, and Anthony Burgess—who were engaging with ideals, style, and alternative world settings rather than the more practical here and now. In *The Fabulators*, Scholes distinguishes his subjects from satirists in that, instead of inducing outrage, they encouraged laughter.

As Vonnegut's status began to rise, his classes became more popular at Iowa and his students began to trust his subversive teaching methods. They grew to appreciate his idiosyncrasies. More than some of his peers, he also displayed genuine concern about their well-being. He often communicated with laughter and would joke with his students. In one class, Vonnegut spoke of how the Crucifixion story in the Bible didn't properly teach compassion because it really just demonstrated that you shouldn't kill someone who was well-connected. According to one of his students, Suzanne McConnell (who, later, became a successful author and writing professor), he laughed so hard that he began to wheeze, prompting a chorus of laughter. Vonnegut later inserted the Crucifixion storyline as a Kilgore Trout novel in *Slaughterhouse-Five*.

Vonnegut was finding a greater sense of belonging, enjoying the school football games and palling around with other faculty, such as Richard Yates, Vance Bourjaily, and Robert Coover, the latter of whom was teaching experimental forms of fiction, including early forays into metafiction. In a decade bursting with upheaval, the novel was getting its own remake with the "death of the author" on everyone's lips.

That spring, Vonnegut was awarded a Guggenheim grant, which he planned to use to fund a trip to East Germany in October to hopefully finish his "famous book about Dresden." He could have stayed at Iowa to teach, but Vonnegut declined the school's offer. He asked Bernard V. O'Hare to join him for an adventure he hoped would provide details and fill out memories of their POW experiences.

But the three-week trip provided little of what Vonnegut was looking for. There were bureaucratic mishaps traveling through East Germany and not much to see other than dull cityscapes and barren landscapes that he likened in the book to Dayton, Ohio. The Germans he spoke with didn't really want to recall the bombing. He tried to look up his old prison guards—the ones he hadn't tried to kill, we'll presume—but no one would talk with him. It wasn't what he was hoping for. It forced him to look inward.

After his return at the end of October 1967, in a letter to Lawrence, Vonnegut wrote, "The trip has simplified the war book for me. *Slaughterhouse-5,* since I have now seen with my own eyes what I was trying to remember." But the truth was that he was more influenced by what he didn't see, which was what Vonnegut suggested to Lawrence when he told him that he now planned to look inside himself to create his story rather than describe what happened on the ground.

IN THE FIRST CHAPTER of *Slaughterhouse-Five,* Vonnegut indicates that he wrote more than five thousand pages by 1965, which he threw out, before arriving at his final draft. At the Lilly library in Indiana, there are at least five hundred pages that appear to come from *Slaughterhouse-Five* drafts.

It is difficult to determine the sequence of these early versions, but, as a whole, they demonstrate Vonnegut's creative progress toward writing about his experience in Dresden, a subject he, for the first time, put in the first person in one of his novels when he added an introduction for the 1966 reissue of *Mother Night*. "135,000 Hansels and Gretels had been baked like gingerbread men," he writes darkly of the firebombing. (Vonnegut never revised his reliance on David Irving's discredited tally despite the number being corrected to approximately 25,000 killed by more conclusive sources. "Does it matter?" That's what Vonnegut told Marc Leeds, author of *The Vonnegut Encyclopedia*.) "If I had been born in Germany, I suppose I would have been a Nazi, bopping Jews and gypsies and Poles around, leaving boots sticking out of snowbanks, warming myself with my secretly virtuous insides. So it goes." This is also the first time he used the famous tagline he would go on to repeat throughout *Slaughterhouse-Five*.

The introduction addresses *Mother Night*'s general subject of ambiguity and its tone of absurdity, but the author's first-person reflections on his connection to the material is incongruous with the fictional tale that follows. Nowhere else does the novel make reference to the author's experience, and by doing so it effectively reframes the story. Vonnegut's upcoming Dresden novel was clearly gestating. And it was the beginning of Vonnegut's signature approach to anchoring his future novels with introductions where Vonnegut, the first-person author, speaks to the reader.

At the Lilly Library, there are two early *Slaughterhouse* attempts that are dramatically different from the final book. One, with the title "Magic Fingers," is about a character who experienced the Dresden bombing, who visits a friend named Bernard

O'Hare during the World's Fair and is fixated on the mechanical beds named in the title. There is another version that runs over 130 pages that has little related to the plotline of *Slaughterhouse* but centers on a character named Billy Pilgrim who is a Pontiac car salesman in the Midwest (glimmers of 1973's *Breakfast of Champions* can be found here), who witnessed the bombing of Dresden. The story, which tells of Pilgrim's relationship with a gay lodger in his home who sells washing machines, doesn't have much dramatic pull.

"I was a hack. I'd write anything to make money, you know," Vonnegut later wrote in *A Man Without a Country.* "And what the hell, I'd seen this thing, I'd been through it, and so I was going to write a hack book about Dresden." Vonnegut found much glee in disparaging himself, especially in print.

"I tried," he added. "But I just couldn't get it right. I kept writing crap."

He's not kidding. I keep coming back to those discarded drafts. He really did write some toilet paper–worthy material. But no judgments! I need you with me on this. I am going to trust that you and I can maintain two potentially inconsistent thought processes in our big brains—appreciate *Slaughterhouse-Five* as it is written and also ferret around how Vonnegut wrote it—without suffering from cognitive dissonance. Or losing a love for the book. Or respect for its creator. He may have been uniquely gifted but it took so much work to make his writing appear almost childlike and off-the-cuff. The evidence is in all those rough drafts. Vonnegut hammered away at making accessibility an art form.

Steve Almond worries that it may be "dirty pool to go mucking through his early efforts," but he does it anyway in his long essay. I do, too. We want to understand the book and the man!

Maybe if we do, we can understand ourselves, right? Almond also writes, "Writers evolve simply because they tire of their own mistakes." I want to see that evolution.

Vonnegut tried this opening: "I have written fiction for fifteen years now. It is too late for me to write anything else. So, even though this book is about things that happened around me, I will have to make them up." He writes, "If I give my word of honor that something is true, then the sentence immediately following usually is fairly true."

Imagine if he tried to carry that throughout the novel. Or there was this one: "I am David McSwan of Hingham, Massachusetts, lying in an unmarked felon's grave in Dresden, where I was shot to death in 1945. And I cry out to the world in nightmare muteness, 'Let there be an end to hate and killing!' Not that I care any more." It was a moralizing clunker he had to get through.

In another discarded draft, he, as the narrator, recalls receiving a letter from a friend, who suggested that together they could write a book about the war that "would make *The Longest Day* look like a minute." Vonnegut takes the high road. "It soon became evident, though that his recollections were far too enthusiastic and violent and romantic for me," he wrote, with the words *far* and *violent* crossed out.

Even as late as October 1966, Vonnegut was still playing with whether or not he should write the story as something less condemning of war and more motivated by financial gain. That month, he admitted in a letter to Knox Burger that he had met with a literary movie agent in Los Angeles who inspired him to write a role for actor Kirk Douglas because a movie adaptation would need to have a strong central character. But it didn't work, he wrote, half ruefully, "because the war I saw wasn't really that way. I am stuck with the fine arts, I guess. Maybe I'll get the Nobel Peace Prize, which is 60 G's."

There are dozens of versions that appear to be much closer to the final book—with no less than eighteen different openings. The lead character is often named Harold Moon or David McSwan, and sometimes Billy Pilgrim. In some, a different character, the mother of a dead POW, challenges the narrator about glorifying war and refers to soldiers as "babies."

There are also versions that include an O'Hare son who is going to fight in Vietnam and one where Billy Pilgrim is gay. He constantly wavers on calling the first section a "preface" or "chapter one."

But, finally, on June 10, 1968, less than ten months after he returned from Dresden, Vonnegut turned in the final draft of *Slaughterhouse-Five*. Weeks before, he had mocked his effort when he wrote in a letter to Scholes, "It sure has been hard. It isn't very long. From now on I am going to follow familiar models and make a lot of dough."

Lawrence was known to have had a very light touch as an editor. Jerome Klinkowitz believes that he may well not have changed as much as a semicolon of the manuscript. With the publication date set for March 1969, Vonnegut's popularity was cresting. By that date, with the help of Lawrence, more than 200,000 mass-market paperback copies of *The Sirens of Titan* and 150,000 *Cat's Cradle* paperbacks had been sold. And, that same month, hundreds of American soldiers died fighting a North Vietnamese offensive in the largest loss of American lives of the war so far. It was an opportune time for an emerging writer with a youthful following to be coming out with an anti-war book.

Much later, explaining how he was finally able to complete

Vonnegut in Concord, New Hampshire, in 1971. Courtesy Library of Congress, Prints and Photographs Division. Photography by Bernard Gotfryd.

his Dresden novel after more than two decades, Vonnegut wrote, "I think the Vietnam War freed me and other writers, because it made our leadership and our motives seem so scruffy and essentially stupid. We could finally talk about something bad that we did to the worst people imaginable, the Nazis. And what I saw, what I had to report, made war look so ugly. You know, the truth can be really powerful stuff."

CHAPTER SIX

A READING OF *SLAUGHTERHOUSE-FIVE*, OR, STOPPING A GLACIER

AFTER ALL THOSE DRAFTS, attempts, and frustrations over so many years, it's incredible that Vonnegut could call *Slaughterhouse-Five* "largely a found object," as he did in a 1973 interview. He described his writing process as "intuitive. There's never any strategy meeting about what you're going to do; you just come to work every day," he said. "I come to work every morning and I see what words come out of the typewriter. I feel like a copyboy whose job is to tear off stories from the teletype machine and deliver them to an editor."

By framing his process this way, he diminishes the cumulative creative achievement that resulted in the book's elliptical, meta-narrative arc lined with comedy, misdirection, time travel, and flights to outer space. There are plenty of academic books (see Notes and Bibliography) dedicated to close textual analysis of *Slaughterhouse-Five* that attest to this. And although the best way to read *Slaughterhouse-Five* is to read *Slaughterhouse-Five*, I am going to provide a highly condensed look at the text of the book in this chapter.

Vonnegut had tried to write the indignant morality tale, but it failed in those countless previous drafts. He had tried to simply "report what I had seen."

In the unpublished essay, "Wailing Shall Be in All Streets," he detailed the atrocities that the Dresden bombing wrought, most viscerally realized by the act of disposing the dead bodies of German civilians. He described how he and his fellow POWs, at first, treated the corpses respectfully. "We had lifted them onto the stretchers with care, laying them out with some semblance of funeral dignity in their last resting place before the pyre," he wrote. But over time, their "awed and sorrowful propriety gave way" to jokes, callousness, and gallows humor. Wearing his heart on his sleeve, Vonnegut makes a strong enough emotional case, but it's not transportive writing. "It is with some regret that I here besmirch the nobility of our airmen, but boys, you killed an appalling lot of women and children," he wrote. "I stand convinced that the brand of justice in which we dealt, wholesale bombings of civilian populations, was blasphemous."

As William Deresiewicz, the author and critic, wrote in *The Nation* magazine in 2012, Vonnegut "needed to surrender that sense of judgment" in order to create an effective approach for *Slaughterhouse-Five*.

The tone Vonnegut came up with is immediately established in the first pages of *Slaughterhouse-Five*, where the author says that his book couldn't have been successfully written. He calls it a "failure" and describes how a movie producer tells him his anti-war book might as well be "an anti-glacier" book, in other words, it was an act of naïveté to try to stop the inevitable. He mocks himself, "an old fart," and his effort, with limericks and self-deprecation.

For readers who have thrown in their lot with Vonnegut and trust his authorial voice, these remonstrations are an ironic recognition of how damn hard it is to get out of bed let alone write a story about war that is true. His ensuing negativity and glib comments are not nihilism or cynicism but dark humor about the inevitability of pain and the inherent flaws of his narrative project.

Vonnegut's rejected University of Chicago thesis paper, "Fluctuations Between Good and Ill Fortune in Simple Tales," which he adapted for his Iowa writing class and later turned into a thirteen-minute, tongue-in-cheek bit for many of his speeches, provides a window into the task he set for himself in writing *Slaughterhouse-Five*. For the talks, he would pull out a blackboard and use chalk to draw a chart with a vertical axis that measured good and ill fortune while the horizontal axis measured the main character's progression through the story. It was reductive and funny: The standard story he called "man in a hole," which starts high, goes low, and ends up higher; "boy meets girl" started in the middle, goes high and then low and then ends up high; "Cinderella" started low and rose when she meets the prince and then falls after the clock strikes twelve and then ends up high again when the prince puts the slipper on her; and so on.

But these rises and falls, Vonnegut said, were in fact "artificial" attempts "to pretend we know more about life than we really do."

In contrast, he charted the trajectory of *Hamlet*. He said that Hamlet starts fairly low on the good–ill fortune axis and then he remains there the entire play, without rising or falling. He drew a straight line across. "We are so seldom told the truth," Vonnegut concludes. "With *Hamlet*, Shakespeare tells us we don't know enough about life to know what the good news and the bad news is."

In writing *Slaughterhouse-Five*, Vonnegut tried to draw his own straight line across.

THE PUBLISHED BOOK OPENS with a neat, spare truth claim that immediately undercuts itself: "All this happened, more or less." The entire first chapter is then told from this voice of the author-narrator, who we have no reason to believe is anyone but Vonnegut himself. He tells of his experiences in World War II and after the war, of his struggle to write the book and even of how he completes it. He tells the biography of the book before it has started, but, in truth, it already has, because we've been reading it.

The entire chapter is the antithesis of conventional writing wisdom that one should show, not tell, a story. The telling becomes the show. Vonnegut tells the reader what the book's about and even what's going to happen, including the climactic killing of Edgar Derby, an American soldier executed by the Nazis for taking a teapot. He also delivers the first and last lines, which are, respectively: "Listen. Billy Pilgrim has become unstuck in time." And: "Poo-tee-weet?"

The first chapter works on many levels. In addition to establishing a seemingly contradictory, alternately earnest and irreverent tone and a pace that jumps in time between memories that are contained in short paragraphs, Vonnegut relays that the tale he is about to tell is an extension of his own real-life story and what happened in Dresden, a forgotten tragedy, worse even than dropping the atomic bomb on Hiroshima in terms of numbers of deaths. (Again: That factually incorrect contrast was something Vonnegut never bothered to clear up.)

Less explicit is the self-portrait he is constructing. He utters those silly limericks and smokes Pall Malls. He drinks late into the night, smells like "mustard gas and roses," talks to his dog, and makes phone calls to ex-girlfriends while his wife sleeps. He also refers to a time when he was a reporter and he saw a dead man who had been mangled by an elevator but it didn't bother him much because he'd "seen lots worse than that in the war."

He comes off as a bit of a sad sack, possibly damaged, but he claims the war made his generation "tough." He laughs at himself but not about war. He is unsettled by war. The central action of the chapter is his visit to his friend Bernard V. O'Hare to see if they can recall memories of the war to help him write the book. They can't come up with much.

Vonnegut describes his drinking and chatting with O'Hare, while the kids played in another room, as being largely unproductive until O'Hare's wife, Mary, displays an irritability that eventually explodes. "You were just babies in the war—like the ones upstairs!" she says. "You'll pretend you were men instead of babies, and you'll be played in the movies by Frank Sinatra and John Wayne or some of those other glamourous, war-loving, dirty old men. And war will look just wonderful, so we'll have a lot more of them. And they'll be fought by babies."

Vonnegut treats it like a revelation. He promises that if he finishes his book, there won't be any characters who could be played by movie stars and that he'll even call it "The Children's Crusade."

But before he starts his story, he articulates the most straightforward message that the book contains: "I have told my sons that they are not under any circumstances to ever take part in massacres, and that the news of massacres of enemies is not to fill them with satisfaction or glee." Also: "I have told them not to work for companies which make massacre machinery, and to express contempt for people who think we need machinery like that."

He then drops several references to let the reader know what else is on his mind. (He sure manages to slip a lot into the first chapter.) He mentions several books, including *Words for the Wind*, a collection by American poet Theodore Roethke; and a book on French novelist Louis-Ferdinand Céline, which gets Vonnegut thinking about Céline's obsession with the passage of time and how "no art is possible without a dance with death."

All of which prompts him to look up tales of destruction in the Bible. He closes the chapter with ruminations about the story of Sodom and Gomorrah and how Lot's wife looked back and was turned into a pillar of salt. The author sees himself as being like her, because he, too, wants to look back, to tell the truth, to stop a glacier, and to dance with death.

THE SECOND CHAPTER STARTS with "Billy Pilgrim has come unstuck in time."

Vonnegut was pretty obsessed with time. Time travel pops up in many of his stories and is a central component of his novel *The Sirens of Titan*. Although in *Slaughterhouse-Five* he doesn't explicitly refer to Mark Twain, whose writing and persona he treasured, Vonnegut employs the same literary device that Twain used in *A Connecticut Yankee in King Arthur's Court* when he launched a nineteenth-century engineer into the sixth century with a knock to his head.

Pilgrim says he jumps between 1963, 1955, 1941, his death and birth and "all the events in between." Vonnegut puts emphasis on the fact that "he says" he's traveling in time by using the phrase repeatedly. The stress on attribution casts doubt on whether or not he is time traveling or if he just says that he is. Pilgrim is not your typical leading man. He is "funny-looking," tall and weak, and we're told he suffered a mental breakdown after serving in World War II, for which he received medical treatment. He doesn't enjoy the time travel, which puts him in a "constant state of stage fright."

Vonnegut briskly unpacks a load of details about Pilgrim's life—he's rich, an optometrist, a widower with two kids, the survivor of a plane crash—and only slows down for what appears to be Pilgrim's mental unraveling after the crash: Pilgrim telling everyone that he's unstuck in time and that he'd been abducted by aliens who put him in a zoo on the planet Tralfamadore, where his abductors mated him with a porn star.

And Pilgrim explains what being unstuck in time, the axis around which the rest of the novel will turn, means. "All moments, past, present, and future, always have existed, always will exist. The Tralfamadorians can look at all the different moments just the way we can look at a stretch of the Rocky Mountains," he writes in a letter. "They can see how permanent all the moments are, and they can look at any moment that interests them. It is just an illusion we have here on Earth that one moment follows another one."

In *Slaughterhouse-Five*'s first chapter, Vonnegut introduced the theme of time and its passing by repeatedly referring to how he can't remember things. And, toward the end of it, he writes of himself being unmoored by a layover during his trip from Germany and being confused by the clocks in his motel. These ruminations lead to his reflecting on Roethke's poem "The Waking," in which the poet writes, "I wake to sleeping, and take my waking slow." The poem raises the liminal divide between being asleep and awake, living in ignorance and gaining knowledge, and life and death.

With the Tralfamadorians, Vonnegut has reconceived time, spatialized it, rendering it like a three-dimensional mobile suspended in the air rather than a sequential stack of cards. As the narrator in the first chapter, he was already jumping in time but more conventionally, as a narrative device. Pilgrim now tells us that, according to the Tralfamadorians, he is able to actually drop in and out of the hopelessly human concept of sequential time. Or so he says.

What function might this reconceptualization of time have for a soldier who has seen the worst of war? "The most important thing I learned on Tralfamadore was that when a person dies he only appears to die," Pilgrim writes in the letter. "Now, when I myself hear that somebody is dead, I simply shrug and say what the Tralfamadorians say about dead people, which is 'so it goes.'" How convenient! He has been relieved of the burden of death.

"So it goes" is repeated over a hundred times in the novel, after every death. Vonnegut later said he was inspired to use "so it goes" as a refrain by Céline's book *Journey to the End of the Night*. "It was a clumsy way of saying what Céline managed to imply," Vonnegut writes in *Palm Sunday*. "In everything he wrote, in effect: 'Death and suffering can't matter nearly as much as I think they do. Since they are so common, my taking them so seriously must mean that I am insane.'"

In Vonnegut's hands, this grim thinking turns into a paradoxically indifferent lament. It is resignation, rage, sorrow, and laughter. What lies beneath it and the many feints, the jokes, the

trippy sci-fi trope of time travel, is a man wrestling with convey-
ing his astonishment at the regularity of pain and death. He was
asked in an interview for *Playboy* in 1973 why he chose to write
his Dresden novel as a work of science fiction.

"The science fiction passages in *Slaughterhouse-Five* are just
like the clowns in Shakespeare," he said. "When Shakespeare figured the audience had had enough of the heavy stuff, he'd let up
a little, bring on a clown or a foolish innkeeper or something like
that, before he'd become serious again. And trips to other planets, science-fiction of an obviously kidding sort, is equivalent to
bringing on the clowns every so often to lighten things up."

Vonnegut created an intricate sci-fi scaffolding with which
readers could experience the suffering of Billy Pilgrim without
either conveniently plugging it into a digestible, clichéd war narrative or overwhelming them with sadness. In other words, if you
strip time travel and Tralfamadorians from Pilgrim's story, and
look at it in summary, it is indeed unbearably bleak.

It starts with him being described as a "tall and weak" only
child alienated from his parents. He pees in his pants when they
visit the Grand Canyon. His mother was "like so many Americans . . . trying to construct a life that made sense from things
she found in gift shops." His dominant memory of his father, who
died in a hunting accident, was of him tossing Pilgrim into the
pool to teach him to sink or swim and just sinking to the bottom
before being saved.

Pilgrim joined the army during World War II as a chaplain's
assistant despite his meek faith. He's a laughingstock without
friends. During the Battle of the Bulge he gets lost with three
other soldiers, one of whom, Roland Weary, abuses him emotionally and physically. The "preposterous" Pilgrim is lethargic

and ready to die but instead he's captured, looking like a "filthy flamingo," by the Germans.

He floats like a simpleton, smiling and hallucinating that he sees halos over the heads of his fellow captured American soldiers through a series of horrors, witnessing corpses and walking with fellow soldiers despairing or dying miserable deaths. Wild Bob, a loopy dying colonel, who mistakes Pilgrim for one of his men, is like a wretched wino raging and raving on skid row; he's broken and terribly sad, but Vonnegut props him up as a comic fool who encourages Pilgrim to come visit him in Cody, Wyoming.

Pilgrim is eventually brought to Dresden, which he finds enchanting before it's destroyed in the air raid. He observes ter-rified German soldiers looking out at the devastation, but he compares them to a barbershop quartet making funny facial expressions. Pilgrim and his fellow POWs are made to dispose of the masses of dead Germans, a process so revolting that one POW dies from dry heaves. But the terror of the experience is inverted and defused by Pilgrim's perception that Dresden has been turned into a "moonscape," a place that doesn't sound half-bad. Vonnegut uses the motif of the lunar landscape—a place that is otherwise peaceful and beautiful—to describe lifelessness. But Pilgrim and his fellow POWs don't belong there. "There were to be no moon men at all," Vonnegut writes.

Throughout his war experiences, the only upstanding, rep-utable American soldier whom Pilgrim gets to know is Edgar Derby. But Vonnegut pulls the rug out from under this tragic figure by sapping the impact of his death by talking about it so baldly with Bernard V. O'Hare in the first chapter. "I think the climax of the whole book will be the execution of poor old Edgar

Derby," he says. "The irony is so great." Which, I suppose, makes it doubly ironic.

And, presto, the climax has been de-climaxed. And when Derby does die on the last page of the book, Vonnegut writes about it as if it was both a foregone conclusion and an afterthought. This is Tralfamadorian timekeeping. There's no moment to grieve because it has happened and it will happen. And the guards leave their posts and Pilgrim is soon wandering free, seemingly blissed out on a horse-drawn wagon. The war is over.

Three years pass and Billy is in a mental hospital where he gets shock treatments. He "didn't really like life at all," we read, but he gets out and marries Valencia, a woman he doesn't want to marry, but he does so anyway, passively. She prods him to talk about his war experience but he can't. About ten years later, he seems to be better adjusted, having become a successful optometrist and a smooth-talking president of the Lions Club.

But he's not OK. Another ten years pass and a doctor has prescribed bed rest for Pilgrim's uncontrolled bouts of weeping. We're reminded he had seen things "worth crying about." He thinks he might be losing his mind when he can't recall what year it is.

But it's 1967, and on his daughter's wedding night Pilgrim can't sleep. He walks outside of his house and is abducted by aliens who take him to the planet Tralfamadore. A year later he survives a plane crash but his skull is fractured, and in the aftermath of the accident, the hysterical Valencia dies on her way to see him in the hospital.

It's unclear how Pilgrim ends up. He gets out of the hospital and begins a campaign to inform humanity of the Tralfamadorian concept of time, to the frustration of his daughter, who believes that his head injury is the cause of his delusions. That's the last seemingly reliable occurrence in his life before his prognostication that he's going to be assassinated by a former fellow POW in a post-apocalyptic 1976, after "angry Chinamen" drop a hydrogen bomb on Chicago.

ABOVE, I'VE PROVIDED a cursory play-by-play of the events of Pilgrim's life and put them in sequence. Rendered this way, we can see that on Vonnegut's fluctuations-in-ill-and-good-fortune chart, Pilgrim's story has no curves. It starts very low and remains there all the way across. But it doesn't feel that way reading the novel because Vonnegut shreds the sequences, reordering and connecting them with time-traveling threads and visits to Tralfamadore. If it weren't for the time travel and science fiction, *Slaughterhouse-Five* would be a terribly grim or deeply cynical version of "War is hell."

In the middle of the novel, the author reveals what he's been doing with a wink and nudge and mind-altering reunion of characters from his other books when Pilgrim is at the mental hospital and he is introduced by fellow veteran Eliot Rosewater to the science fiction novels of author Kilgore Trout, Vonnegut's fictional avatar. Like Pilgrim, Rosewater, also the protagonist from *God Bless You, Mr. Rosewater*, finds life "meaningless" after his war experience. The two men find solace, we are told, in Trout's novels. "So they were trying to re-invent themselves and their universe. Science fiction was a big help," our narrator says.

They're not the only ones reinventing their lives with science fiction. Vonnegut is referring to himself, the guy rewriting his personal war story as a far-out, speculative tale.

Vonnegut begins reinventing Pilgrim's story of woe by inserting time travel in 1944, when he is deliriously lost in the woods, wanting to die, before being captured by the Germans. From then on, he bounces in time from his past to his future so there is no present. Or it is always present. According to the Tralfamadorian concept of time, we are all stuck in all of the moments of our lives, like bugs trapped in amber.

On Pilgrim's daughter's wedding night, when he is abducted by the Tralfamadorians, they take him in a large flying saucer with portholes around its rim. He's placed in a geodesic dome with furniture and observed by the Tralfamadorians as if he's an animal in a zoo. He's about as happy there as he was on Earth, he tells them.

Pilgrim tries to inform the Tralfamadorians about the atrocities of war that he's witnessed, but the aliens are indifferent. They explain that they have horrible wars as well but that none of it matters because of their concept of time. It's all happening at once. So they prefer to focus on their happy, non-war days.

The Tralfamadorians want to see humans have sex, so they abduct a porn star named Montana Wildhack, who, after initially freaking out about her situation, eventually sleeps with Pilgrim, who describes the experience as "heavenly." She becomes pregnant, they have a child, and Pilgrim seems relatively content.

ALTHOUGH THE BOOK DOES NOT SPEND a lot of time on Tralfamadore, it's enough to turn a sad story about a traumatized war veteran into a mind-bending trip. A reader could come away feeling tickled rather than having been tossed a hand grenade. But throughout the book, Vonnegut gives clues that the time traveling and Tralfamadorians are not real and are simply a product of the damaged mind of Pilgrim, a twisted Dorothy in an Oz of his own creation. What happens on Tralfamadore has physical corollaries in Pilgrim's earthbound existence.

Toward the end of the novel, Pilgrim enters a porno shop near Times Square where he encounters much of what ends up in his Tralfamadorian experience. He reads a Kilgore Trout novel in which a man and a woman are abducted by aliens and put in a zoo to be observed on a faraway planet. He reads another Trout book in which a man travels in time. And then he notices a porno mag that asks, "What really became of Montana Wildhack?"

Earlier in the book, Pilgrim reads another Trout novel in which an alien is shaped "very much" like Tralfamadorians, which are about two feet tall, green, with suction cups similar to "plumber's friends," or toilet plungers.

Another clue is how there are recurrences throughout the novel. These point the reader to consider if these are more than mere coincidences and that not everything that is happening is, in fact, happening, making Pilgrim's reality more brittle. At different stages of his life, Pilgrim's frozen feet are ivory and blue, as are the feet of the dead American GIs. The POW train car is painted orange and black, as is the wedding tent of Pilgrim's daughter. There's the barbershop quartet on the plane that crashes and also at his anniversary party; it reminds him of the Nazi guards who appeared to him to be a similar, if macabre, group of merry singers. Roland Weary, the American soldier who abuses Pilgrim, imagines he and two fellow soldiers are like the Three Musketeers. There are two mentions of other characters eating Three Musketeers chocolate bars.

Also, Vonnegut provides mirror bookends by describing his breath in the first chapter as smelling like mustard gas and roses. He uses the same evocative way to describe the smell of the Dresden citizens' rotting corpses in the final chapter. Similar to the time traveling, the recurrences create a mesmerizing, surreal effect that lifts the reader above the painful details of the story.

And Vonnegut adds yet another layer to the kaleidoscope by breaking the fourth wall periodically. In between the first and last chapter, Vonnegut inserts himself into Pilgrim's story four times.

"I was there," the narrator says of himself after Pilgrim is captured and made to march by the Germans. In yet another recurrence, Pilgrim also says, "I was there," to inform his hospital roommate that he was at Dresden.

The second time that the narrator steps in, he mentions that he could have the same epitaph as Billy: "Everything was beautiful and nothing hurt." And then when Pilgrim is a POW surrounded by other POWs experiencing terrible bouts of diarrhea, Vonnegut, as the narrator and author, writes that he was there, shitting his brains out: "That was I. That was me. That was the author of this book."

The fourth time occurs when Pilgrim approaches Dresden and the narrator says, "Oz" (wink, wink, nudge, nudge; he might as well be screaming, "Billy is Dorothy!"), referring to the grand beauty of the city. "That was I. That was me. The only other city I'd ever seen was Indianapolis, Indiana," he writes. By the last chapter of the book, Vonnegut appears to be continuing where he left off in the first chapter, reflecting on the writing of the book. He says he just finished writing it days after the assassination of Robert F. Kennedy and two months after Martin Luther King Jr. was killed. He writes of these events, of his own father and Pilgrim, as if they're all on the same plane of actuality.

It's confusing if you don't give in to it. But if the reader accepts that the book treats fiction like nonfiction and nonfiction like fiction, then it totally works.

That is what Vonnegut could do with fiction. Of course, there is an actual history wherein real things really happened to Vonnegut during World War II.

CHAPTER SEVEN

WHAT REALLY HAPPENED TO VONNEGUT IN WORLD WAR II, OR, THE WAR PARTS, ANYWAY

VONNEGUT HAS BEEN COMPARED to Mark Twain; he did indeed revere the great nineteenth-century humorist and social critic, who was also from the Midwest. Vonnegut named his son Mark. And it's been said he emulated him by growing his signature drooping mustache. In *Palm Sunday*, Vonnegut wrote of Twain: "He himself was the most enchanting American at the heart of each of his tales. We can forgive this easily, but he managed to imply that the reader was enough like him to be his brother."

Vonnegut follows Twain in constructing a similarly powerful presence for himself in *Slaughterhouse-Five*. Although Pilgrim plods listlessly through his story, we know that the character is under the firm control of the author, who, despite some late-night drunken phone dialing, seems to be pretty much all right. Vonnegut is the true protagonist of the novel, the one who carries the reader from the first to the last page. And he has made it to 1968, maybe a little bit sad, but "extremely well-to-do," he tells us, and having had lots of nice moments to reflect on. Plus, he finally finished this book—even if he disparages it.

The realness of the author who doubles up as the lead character of the book poses interesting questions about how really real

Slaughterhouse-Five is when Vonnegut writes, "All this happened, more or less. The war parts, anyway, are pretty much true...." How much does what the author says he went through and what Pilgrim went through (which may or may not overlap) actually correlate with historical facts?

When it comes to the war parts, most of it, actually. Vonnegut was faithful to the facts of what happened to his unit. The most over-the-top, absurdly tragicomic elements of Billy Pilgrim's war story—that his entry into combat coincided with the worst American defeat (in terms of casualties) of World War II just as it was about to end, that he was awkwardly, immediately captured by the Germans, and then that he survived the horrific Allied firebombing of the beautiful, ancient city of Dresden because he was preserved in a meat locker meant for carcasses under a slaughterhouse—actually happened to Vonnegut. And the other general World War II facts from *Slaughterhouse-Five* hew very closely to what happened to Vonnegut and the other members of the 423rd Regiment, starting with their surrender in the forest (as described by Derby), the deprivations of the forced march, the insufferable conditions in the train boxcars, the shower delousing, and so on.

Pilgrim's POW experiences have been corroborated by other members of Vonnegut's regiment, from the highly organized and well-fed British soldiers who really put on a show for the Americans, to their labor at a malt syrup factory and the surreal imprisonment in a slaughterhouse. They also recalled the bombing of Dresden, although they, too, couldn't recall exact details. Same goes for the cleaning up of dead Germans. And their freedom, from the guards wandering off to the horse-drawn wagon, happened to Vonnegut just as they did to Pilgrim. There are even photos of Vonnegut sitting in the back of the wagon just as Pilgrim describes it.

As for the main characters, the author begins the book by saying that he really knew a guy who was shot for stealing a teapot. This is mostly accurate. It is generally agreed upon that the "poor Edgar Derby" character is based on Michael Palaia, a soldier from Pennsylvania in the 423rd Regiment. He was one of the two American POWs kept in Schlachthof-Fünf who died during their internment.

Like his fellow Americans, Palaia was forced to clean up the dead and rubble from the ruins. The POWs knew that stealing could be punished with death, but they had been starved for so many weeks, many were willing to take the risk. They would eat food they found in the cellars of bombed-out buildings in Dresden. German guards would turn a blind eye or would accept bribes.

According to interviews with the POWs published in *Shadows of Slaughterhouse Five*, a series of firsthand accounts compiled by former POW Ervin Szpek and his son-in-law Frank Idzikowski, Palaia came upon a jar of string beans (some say it was preserves), which he hid in his recycled Russian coat. But a member of the SS had Palaia searched and discovered the jar. Palaia was told to sign a document, which he probably didn't understand, and then given a quick trial. He and a Russian prisoner, who had also been accused of plundering, were brought to a training area with four American POWs and the same number of Russians. Palaia and the Russian were shot by German soldiers and buried in graves dug by their respective comrades.

It was Palaia's execution that Vonnegut described to his family after returning home in July of 1945, before bursting into tears and crying, "The sons of bitches! The sons of bitches!"

In Vonnegut's book, he changes a few details, including Palaia's name, and most vividly turning the jar of string beans into a teapot. But even that latter embellishment had some corollary in reality. In *Shadows of Slaughterhouse Five,* two American POWs spoke of a porcelain figurine, which Dresden was famous for, being picked up by an American soldier who was also an Indiana high school principal.

When Vonnegut fictionalized Palaia into being Derby, he made him the most conventional literary character in *Slaughterhouse-Five.* "There are almost no characters in this story, and almost no dramatic confrontations, because most of the people in it are so sick and so much the listless playthings of enormous forces. One of the main effects of war, after all, is that people are discouraged from being characters. But old Derby was a character now," Vonnegut writes. He describes what is "probably the finest moment in his life," when Derby confronts an American traitor, Howard Campbell, who joined the Nazis and appeals to the American POWs to switch sides. Derby insults him and speaks movingly about American ideals.

John Wayne or Frank Sinatra may not have been able to convincingly play Derby in a movie version, but Henry Fonda (who actually starred in 1965's *Battle of the Bulge*) wouldn't have been too much of a stretch. Derby is an older soldier, an Indianapolis high school teacher(!) who is honorable and shows compassion. He pulled strings so that he could fight for his country despite being forty-four years old. (Come to think of it, Tom Hanks played a similar teacher turned squad leader in *Saving Private*

Ryan when he was forty-one years old.) Derby cares for Roland Weary as he dies in a train boxcar and looks after Pilgrim when he's in the POW infirmary. Despite a lethargic voting process, Derby is elected to lead the American POWs.

A good snapshot of how Vonnegut struggled creatively to write about his experiences during the war is his development of the Derby-Palaia character. He began with the early story, "Atrocity Story." Told from the first person, it appears to be an almost entirely nonfictional account of Palaia's case. The narrator tells of himself and three other recently freed POWs who report the case of Palaia, whose name is changed to Steve Malotti, to officers at a War Crimes Commission tent at Camp Lucky Strike in France, where Vonnegut actually recuperated after being held prisoner. They tell the story of Malotti's execution for stealing a jar of beans to the officers, who dismiss it as not being a war crime because he was accused of plundering and given a trial, no matter how unjust or unfair that may have been.

Despite the uninspired storytelling, "Atrocity Story" dabbles in the dark irony that ends up in *Slaughterhouse-Five*; the discouraging War Crimes officers express relief that Malotti's execution will be avenged by the Russians, who will execute every "Jerry" within fifty miles of where Malotti and the Russian soldier were killed.

Vonnegut made multiple attempts at constructing a Palaia-like character as the protagonist of *Slaughterhouse-Five*. At the Lilly Library, there are discarded drafts in which Vonnegut used the names David McSwan (Vonnegut lifted the name from an actual Cape Cod local, a tough-guy archetype he delighted in pillorying) and Harold Moon as his protagonist who is killed for plundering. In some of those versions, it is McSwan/Moon's grieving mother, as opposed to Mary O'Hare, who asks the author/narrator/Vonnegut not to make her son into a character that could be played by Frank Sinatra.

"Don't pretend you were men back then. Tell the truth: You were just babies. When they tied David to a stake and shot him, that was a baby they shot," Mrs. McSwan says when the author visits her on a trip with his daughter and her friend. Mrs. McSwan bangs around in the kitchen to show her anger at Vonnegut and his war-book project, just as Mary O'Hare does in the published version.

It is evident that Vonnegut worked and reworked this section countless times, including placing the sequence in a surreal episode in the middle of the book when an old drunk calls Billy Pilgrim in the middle of the night and tells him about what Mary O'Hare said to him. The "old drunk," of course, is supposed to be Vonnegut, so he had himself calling his fictional character. What fun! But he ultimately placed it in the first chapter as something the narrator-author had actually experienced.

The other American POW from the 423rd Regiment who died during their internment was Edward "Joe" Crone, an engineering student from upstate New York. Vonnegut grappled, creatively and personally, with how to write a character inspired by Crone. There's a draft of *Slaughterhouse-Five* at the Lilly that appears to have been written while Vonnegut was still in Iowa, which means he worked on it between the fall of 1965 and the spring of 1967. It opens with the following dedication, written in pencil: "In memory of private Joe Crone, who died in Dresden, before our eyes, and who was buried by the Germans in a snow-white civilian suit made of crinkly white paper. Row, row,

row your boat, gently down the stream. Merrily, merrily, merrily, merrily, life is but a dream."

But Vonnegut changed his mind about openly connecting Crone to the novel. In fact, the author kept the connection secret for twenty-five more years, until the 1990s.

According to soldiers in the 423rd Regiment, Crone was a gawky young private who didn't seem to belong in the army. In training, he kept losing his equipment, which would fall from his backpack. He looked, according to Vonnegut, like "a filthy flamingo," which is how he describes Pilgrim. Crone, who talked of entering the ministry, didn't fit in well with his fellow soldiers. And when he was a POW, he became more insular. He would trade food for cigarettes, indifferent to his own hunger, which everyone knew was foolish. But he was taken advantage of. He began to waste away and he seemed to give up on life and let himself slowly die. Just weeks before the war ended, Crone died of malnutrition. One POW said Crone had died "of a broken heart."

It was a sad, dispiriting death and it stuck with Vonnegut, particularly the white paper suit that the Germans buried him in. Crone had given up, Vonnegut later said, "because life made absolutely no sense to him. And he was right. It wasn't making any sense at all. So he didn't want to pretend he understood it any more, which is more than the rest of us did. We pretended we understood it."

IT'S HARD TO CATCH, but Vonnegut was being earnest in that opening line of the book. One can confidently say that most of what is described in *Slaughterhouse-Five* during the war—not including minor character details and interactions or Pilgrim's mind trips—actually happened. But can we put a number on that? Seventy-five percent? That would be about as valid as saying Edgar Derby is 60 percent Michael Palaia or Pilgrim himself is 50 percent Joe Crone and 50 percent Kurt Vonnegut.

As Jerome Klinkowitz would instruct us, literary creations are fluid and shouldn't be broken down to an assemblage of parts that can be tabulated and individually sourced. How much of Pilgrim's despair and confusion did Vonnegut feel during the war and after? Even the author could not say that. It's a little bit like asking how much any one of us is like the people who raised us. We may have a sense of the answer, but it's impossible to come up with a definite one.

It took Vonnegut twenty-three years to construct a postmodern fable that fun house–mirrored his experiences. He purposefully conflated his authorial presence with that of his fictional characters. How much is really real and not real in *Slaughterhouse-Five* is part of a creative game; embracing ambiguity was Vonnegut's way of telling the story.

It works for the novel, but it obscures an understanding of how much of Pilgrim's suffering was also experienced by Vonnegut, which is bound to come to mind for many readers. "During the war, Vonnegut kept it together externally. I bet internally it was a much more chaotic and messy story," says Vonnegut superfan Steve Almond, who believes that Pilgrim personified some "inner part of Vonnegut that was psychically, completely bewildered" by his war experiences.

"Billy Pilgrim was his way to write about the part of him that was inwardly chaotic," Almond adds. "The act of writing the book was a sort of mastery over that chaos."

Vonnegut believed in the corrective power of stories. "My reason for writing is unfortunately in line with Hitler's and Stalin's," he snarked in 1970. "I think writers should serve their society."

And not just the general populace, but also for himself: "I did what I did without knowing what I was doing," Vonnegut said in a 2002 interview. "Until I read a book called *The Writer and Psychoanalysis*, written by a psychiatrist named Edmund Bergler, who once worked in New York and treated mainly writers. I think he was right in his diagnosis that writers and artists are fortunate because they can cope with their neuroses in their day-to-day work."

Vonnegut denied that he had any major neuroses to cope with regarding the war. The only damage he was willing to concede was the impact of being "very hungry" for six months. Even that—he went from being 175 pounds to 134 pounds—he belittled. He had these harrowing experiences, and he wrote a book about practically the same exact experiences causing his protagonist to go into a severe mental tailspin . . . but not him, he'd say.

In his books, Vonnegut's characters often find solace from their pain in telling and hearing stories. In *Slaughterhouse-Five*, the doomed, embittered Roland Weary fantasizes relaying to his family what Vonnegut calls "Weary's version of the true war story." The character imagines telling them that he and two scouts become buddy-heroes, the Three Musketeers, which becomes a story within Vonnegut's story. Weary is delusional but it makes him feel better. And after we're told Rosewater and Pilgrim tried to reinvent themselves with science fiction, Rosewater informs Pilgrim that "everything there was to know about life" was in Dostoevsky's *The Brothers Karamazov*. But, for Rosewater, "that

Vonnegut (third from left, with hands in pockets) with fellow
American POWs after they were released in May 1945.
Courtesy of Vicki Jones Cole.

isn't enough anymore," so he tells a psychiatrist in the mental hospital, "I think you guys are going to have to come up with a lot of wonderful *new* lies, or people just aren't going to want to go on living."

If these acts of storytelling are indications that his characters are suffering, then the same logic could be extended to the author himself, no? His wartime experiences—surrendering to the enemy, experiencing starvation and imprisonment, witnessing death and suffering—can all be described as traumatizing events, as at least two of his children say. But I am not ready to play Vonnegut's armchair psychologist, especially without him around. To better understand Billy Pilgrim and the author who created him, we need to next place them in the larger historical context of war trauma.

CHAPTER EIGHT
A HISTORY OF WAR TRAUMA

ON JANUARY 31, 1945, while Vonnegut was starving but surviving in a Dresden POW camp, American private Eddie Slovik was being shot to death by an American firing squad in a small town in eastern France. Slovik, the first American soldier to be executed for desertion since the Civil War, was an ex-con from Detroit who had initially been deferred from military service but was called up when the army lowered its standards to fill its ranks as the war dragged on. In the summer of 1944, Slovik had engaged in his first battle in France and was so terrified by the shelling and heavy gunfire that, he said, he became paralyzed and got lost from his unit.

He confessed to desertion, saying that he was "so scared" with "nerves and trembling" and that he would desert again rather than face combat. He requested to be stationed away from the fighting but was denied. Slovik was given opportunities to change his mind, but he didn't, preferring the stockade to combat.

Of the ten million World War II inductees, forty thousand American soldiers deserted. Of those, fewer than three thousand were court-martialed and forty-nine were condemned to death during the war but no executions were carried out. Slovik had good reason to think his punishment would be imprisonment until the war ended.

Just before Slovik was killed, the attending chaplain said to him, "Eddie, when you get up there, say a little prayer for me." Slovik replied, "Okay, Father. I'll pray that you don't follow me too soon."

Without commentary or color, Vonnegut includes Eddie Slovik in *Slaughterhouse-Five* by having Pilgrim find a copy of 1954's *The Execution of Private Slovik* by William Bradford Huie, and he reads a short section in which a staff judge advocate affirms the death sentence "to maintain that discipline upon which alone an army can succeed against the enemy." Vonnegut leaves it at that.

I want to take this moment before we go through an entire history of war trauma to acknowledge the remarkable grace with which Vonnegut can allude to that same history with nothing more than a wisp of a paragraph, a barely-there reference to the real-life Slovik. There is so much that underlies the words on Vonnegut's pages and his seemingly insignificant characters.

Eighteen months before Slovik was killed, General George S. Patton, who was leading the American campaign into Italy, visited an army hospital where he met Charles Kuhl, a carpet-layer from Indiana who was suffering from "psychoneurosis anxiety" as well as malaria. When Patton asked Kuhl what was wrong with him, Kuhl replied, "I guess I can't take it," and that he was "nervous." Patton had a fit, calling Kuhl a coward, slapping him with his gloves, and demanding that he be sent to the front.

A week later, Patton was introduced to Private Paul Bennett from South Carolina in another hospital. Bennett had become "confused, weak and listless" after a comrade had been severely injured. When he struggled to come to attention, Patton asked how he was injured. Bennet replied that it was his "nerves," prompting Patton to slap Bennett around and yell at him, "Your nerves, hell. You're a goddamned coward, you yellow son-of-a-bitch!"

In addition to being a successful commander, Patton was famous for being headstrong and impolitic, and General Dwight Eisenhower reassigned him for these and other acts. It was reported that President Franklin Delano Roosevelt received hundreds of letters regarding the general's reprimand for slapping the battle-fatigued soldiers—most of them in support of Patton. The general remained an essential part of the American military leadership through the defeat of Germany in May 1945.

There may be no mention of Patton in *Slaughterhouse-Five*, but Vonnegut created two Patton-like stand-ins, otherwise minor characters who embody his blood-and-guts machismo. There's a former major who gives a speech at a luncheon at the Lions Club, where he says the United States should bomb Vietnam into the Stone Age. Pilgrim goes limp when talking to the former major, and then he goes home and weeps in bed.

And there is the buffoonish retired brigadier Air Force general, Bertram Copeland Rumfoord, who shares a hospital room with Pilgrim after Pilgrim survives the plane crash. Rumfoord is writing a history of World War II. He champions military might without reflection; the hospital staff consider him "hateful," "conceited," and "cruel" because he thinks that weak people, such as Pilgrim, should die. Rumfoord tells Pilgrim that the Dresden bombing "had to be done." And Pilgrim meekly agrees; "I know," he says. "Everybody has to do exactly what he does."

"I could carve a better man out of a banana," Rumfoord says of Pilgrim, slightly misquoting the pugilist president Theodore Roosevelt.

EDDIE SLOVIK AND GENERAL PATTON are part of America's long, twisted history with war trauma that Vonnegut, either explicitly or implicitly, was responding to when he wrote *Slaughterhouse-Five*. Over the years, the military's definition of the mental effects of war has come in different forms and with different names. And although perceptions of it have evolved over history, there are consistent threads. To better understand Vonnegut's perception of the casualties of war, Vonnegut's son, Mark, suggested I read 1994's *Achilles in Vietnam: Combat Trauma and the Undoing of Character*, an innovative approach to the subject written by Veterans Affairs psychiatrist Jonathan Shay, who recognized that his Vietnam veteran patients suffered traumatic symptoms that could be found in Homer's *Iliad*.

In the nearly three-thousand-year-old epic poem, the Greeks are at war with the Trojans. The Greek king Agamemnon is in conflict with his greatest warrior, Achilles. Agamemnon unjustly takes from Achilles one of the spoils of the war, a captive woman, for himself, which is a great insult to the soldier. (What this all means for the woman doesn't merit an iota of consideration, sadly.) This betrayal by an authority is what Shay calls "moral injury," and it causes a physiological response in Achilles, which is to go into a rage akin to the berserk response that Shay observed in many contemporary soldiers. Things don't get better for Achilles; his best friend, Patroclus, puts on Achilles's armor and is killed by the Trojan warrior Hector, causing Achilles to fall into despair. He grieves the loss of his friend and is racked by guilt. He then goes on a destructive rage and, after finally killing Hector, he debases his body in another berserk act. Afterward, Achilles weeps and despairs over the cruelties of war.

What Achilles and Vietnam soldiers share, Shay told me, is psychological injury from war. "PTSD is a physioneurosis. It's really in the body and the mind," he said. "But I've tried to lower the status of PTSD as the only bad thing that can happen to a person in war. I've introduced another kind of injury: moral injury." What Shay wants to emphasize is that the betrayal of "what's right" can have a deeply existential, damaging effect on a soldier's mind.

Jump to the seventeenth century, when modern thinking about war trauma can be traced to the original meaning of the word *nostalgia*, a term created in 1688 by Swiss doctor Johannes Hofer to describe soldiers who have an unnerving longing to return home from war. *Nostros* comes from the Greek word for *homecoming* and *algos* is from the word *pain*.

Eighteenth-century military doctors often recommended sick leave as a treatment for nostalgia, but some proposed more aggressive measures. French doctor Jourdan Le Cointe wrote that telling an ailing soldier that he would be treated with a hot iron to the stomach should set him straight.

Later, during the Napoleonic Wars, French soldiers who were perpetually terrified by the sound of the wind from cannonballs flying overhead were said to have *vent du boulet*, or "cannonball wind," syndrome.

At the same time that military technology was developing new ways to kill more soldiers, the advent of the railroad era in the nineteenth century was tarnished by catastrophic train crashes that incurred mass casualties, which led to another new condition, "railway spine," coined by British surgeon John Eric

Erichsen. He observed that victims of such train accidents would develop persistent symptoms of pain, nervousness, and other debilitating conditions rooted in the spine but also manifested in the brain.

Seemingly related, during the American Civil War, Philadelphia military doctor Jacob Mendez Da Costa keyed into a set of symptoms he saw in Union soldiers—breathlessness, heart palpitations, headaches, and difficulty sleeping—that he called "irritable heart." Da Costa published his findings in 1871, establishing an early connection between the functions of the mind and the body.

There was an increasing awareness of the condition, which was referred to as Soldier's Heart or Da Costa's syndrome, when journalist and novelist Stephen Crane, who was born after the Civil War, chose to write what he later called "a psychological portrayal of fear" about the war, something he believed he had an intuitive feel for because of his early days engaging with the "rage of conflict on the football field." Crane's *Red Badge of Courage*, published in 1894, focuses on the experiences of Henry Fleming, a young soldier from the Union Army who is terrified of combat and worries about whether or not he will flee the fighting instead of earn his red badge of courage, the battle wound that will prove his worthiness in war. He does in fact run away from his first skirmish, desert his unit, get banged up by one of his own comrades, and eventually return to battle, where he has a berserk episode and putatively proves his valor. The book was a huge hit, and its realistic approach—many readers believed Crane had fought in the war—helped shape Americans' understanding of the strains of war on the mind of the soldier.

Advances in medicine and the tools of war prompted more new thinking about soldiers' mental injuries during World

War I. The fighting was unprecedented in its devastation. A battery of French 75mm field guns could annihilate ten acres of land in less than fifty seconds. A single machine gun could deliver more than five hundred rounds in a minute, capable of mowing soldiers down in a range of thousands of yards. And as if the efficiency of those killing machines weren't enough, all sides of the conflict made infamous use of chemical weapons. Despite previous international treaties against poisonous weapons, they used chlorine gas, phosgene, and mustard gas to cataclysmic effect, causing suffocation, blindness, chemical burning, and, eventually, death.

Still, it has been estimated that most of the dying, 60 percent of the war's ten million military fatalities, was caused by the most psychologically damaging weaponry of all: artillery projectile bombing, or shelling. And *shell shock* was the new term, coined in 1915 in Britain just six months into the war, for the incapacitating effect on soldiers being subjected to the barrage of modern bombs.

British medical officers saw soldiers coming into hospitals with consistent mentally induced symptoms—trembling, headaches, tinnitus, confusion, loss of memory, and sleep disorders—in addition to more severe physical symptoms, such as locked limbs and the inability to stand up. These shell-shocked soldiers were given "wound stripes" on their uniforms when the initial thinking was that the impact of the bombs was concussive—literally shaking the soldiers' brains.

But it became apparent that soldiers who had not even been near bombing were also displaying similar symptoms, causing confusion among the medical units. These indirectly affected casualties were then referred to as suffering "neurasthenia," a weakness of nerves, and considered to be more akin to an illness than a physical injury.

As their understanding of the related ailments evolved, British medical doctors tried to avoid the term *shell shock*. But despite their desire to differentiate between the symptoms, *shell shock* was the all-encompassing name most often used for soldiers who were similarly afflicted, whether or not they were exposed to bombing. In 1917, British soldiers admitted to psychiatric hospitals were given the diagnosis of either "shell shock (wound)" or "shell shock (nervous)," depending on whether or not they'd been directly exposed to artillery.

Treatments for shell shock ranged from bed rest and the "talking cure" to hypnotism and electric shock therapy. The seriousness of the condition was not lost on the British. There aren't definitive numbers of how many soldiers suffered shell shock, with estimates ranging from 4 to 20 percent. (A vast trove of British World War I military records were destroyed by a fire caused by Germany's air bombing of London during World War II; additionally, a majority of US records of army service members from 1912 to 1960 were also destroyed by a fire in 1973.)

Word of the ravages of shell shock carried over to the US military, which enlisted Thomas Salmon, the medical director of the National Committee for Mental Hygiene, to come up with a defense for its troops. Salmon was dispatched to Europe to research the condition in 1917, the same year that the United States entered the war.

Salmon reported that "the psychological basis of the war neuroses [is] escape from an intolerable situation in real life to one made tolerable." The causes could be fear, horror, and "revulsion against the ghastly duties which sometimes must be performed."

He noted that the "constitutionally neurotic" were prone to the condition but that there was also the "striking fact" that "apparently normal" men fell victim to the condition as well. The first order of business was then to screen new recruits for signs that they might have mental conditions that would make them susceptible to shell shock, a mandate that came from the top when General John J. Pershing, the commander of the American forces, complained about the "prevalence of mental disorders" among his replacement troops. Ultimately, the US armed forces rejected approximately 2 percent of inductees based on mental fitness, a number both psychiatrists and military officials agreed was too low.

During the war, Salmon was able to establish a psychiatric response plan with five key principles—immediacy, proximity, expectancy, simplicity, and centrality—for admitting ailing American troops, but it was difficult to treat soldiers spread out over Europe. According to Salmon, treatment had to happen before chronic symptoms developed; it had to be near the front line and the soldier's unit; there should be optimism for a prompt cure instilled by persuasive psychotherapy; simplicity meant bed rest and therapy that didn't dig into childhood traumas or the like; and centrality meant an organization that efficiently moved the patient from the front to the rear and that treatment was uniform from all caregivers.

But Salmon received criticism for his occupational therapy approach. One of Salmon's superiors in the US, Pearce Bailey, the head of neurology and psychiatry for the army, believed Salmon was too "sentimental." Bailey preferred the French military hospitals' punitive treatments—solitary confinement, threats of electrical shock—for its soldiers.

Major Frederick Parsons, the commanding officer of Salmon's flagship intake center, Base Hospital No. 117, also had a negative view of Salmon's approach. After the war, Parsons defended the success of the psychiatric treatment by the United States, citing the low number—5 percent—of soldiers who didn't recover. Referring to them as a negligible problem that was "easily absorbed into American society," Parsons wrote that "a war neurosis which persists is not a creditable disease to have, as it indicates in practically every case a lack of the soldierly qualities which have distinguished the Allied Armies."

"No one should be permitted to glorify himself as a case of 'shell shock,'" Parsons wrote in a letter to a newspaper in 1919. "It should become widely known that a persistent war neurosis is not something of which to be proud. It is not the same as an honorable wound."

The military and medical opinion was far from resolved on the issue of trauma. There were questions about whether or not soldiers were "malingerers" claiming symptoms to avoid service or to receive disability. Any doubt painted the truly wounded with the same brush. France, unlike Great Britain and the United States, was particularly harsh, declining to provide pensions for victims of shell shock.

The cultural response to shell shock victims was also ambiguous. It didn't help that there was censorship on both sides of the Atlantic, silencing recognition of the toll of the war. The Great War poets of Great Britain, who had a popular following at the beginning of the war, were notably of the "blood and glory" variety, articulating love for country and the glory of sacrifice. "Much suffering shall cleanse thee," wrote Britain's poet laureate Robert Bridges in *Wake Up, England* in 1914.

By the end of the war, though, English poets such as Wilfred Owen and Siegfried Sassoon gave lyrical voice to the horrors of war. Owen's most famous poem, "Dulce et Decorum Est," tells of a soldier dying miserably from poison gas: "If you could hear, at every jolt, the blood / Come gargling from the froth-corrupted lungs, / Obscene as cancer, bitter as the cud / Of vile, incurable sores on innocent tongues."

The two soldiers wrote of shell shock; they had in fact met at the Craiglockhart psychiatric hospital in Scotland. Both wrote of the enduring pain that they and their fellow soldiers endured, most notably in Sassoon's "Survivors" ("Men who went out to battle, grim and glad / Children, with eyes that hate you, broken and mad") and Owen's "Mental Cases," both written in 1917.

This literary response to World War I's shell shock phenomenon coincided with leaps in the field of psychiatry, which had been conceived in the early nineteenth century. Mental illness had been a subject of consideration as far back as ancient India and Greece, but it wasn't until the late 1800s that psychiatry clued into how traumatic events in a person's life could live on separately from memory and materialize as an intense emotional reaction, such as aggressive behavior or physical pain.

In 1893, Sigmund Freud and Josef Breuer published a paper on hysteria in which they wrote, "The . . . memory of the trauma . . . acts like a foreign body which long after its entry must be regarded as an agent that is still at work." As psychoanalysis developed, Freud continued to study trauma. In 1921's *Psychoanalysis and the War Neuroses*, for which he wrote an introduction, Freud noted how the pervasiveness of war neuroses had abetted the spread of psychoanalysis among the military medical establishment. He considered some symptomatic soldiers to be damaged by a battle between their peacetime egos and their war-time egos. But there was disagreement about the applicability of the Austrian's work to shell shock. In Britain, among the findings of 1922's *Report of the War Office Committee of Enquiry into "Shell-Shock,"* there was the recommendation to not treat with "psycho-analysis in the Freudian sense."

In the United States, a billion dollars was spent by the government to care for World War I veterans with psychiatric disabilities between 1923 and 1940. By 1940, three out of five VA hospital beds were for veterans with neuropsychiatric conditions. And yet, the United States entered into World War II without a treatment plan for trauma or a comprehensive criteria for detecting neuropsychiatric disabilities. Nevertheless, recruits were screened for potential mental disorders as well as other conditions, including neurosis and maladjustment. The military also hoped to reject gay men, believing that homosexuality could destroy troop morale. Of fifteen million possible soldiers, 1,875,000 were declared unfit, a rejection rate of 12 percent, which was approximately five times that of World War I.

In 1941, New York psychoanalyst (and former patient of Freud's) Abram Kardiner published *The Traumatic Neuroses of War*, warning that war would damage men mentally and that without early treatment their condition could become chronic. His diagnosis was that, with war neuroses, "the subject acts as if the original traumatic situation were still in existence and engages in protective devices which failed on the original occasion. This means in effect that his conception of the outer world and his conception of himself have been permanently altered."

Kardiner complained about how the military's medical responders weren't learning from past research. In fact, the US

Army initially ignored his and Salmon's earlier directives to treat afflicted soldiers promptly and close to the front line. The military assumed that soldiers inclined to war neuroses had been screened out when they enlisted, ignoring the evidence that even "normal" soldiers were susceptible. Instead, symptomatic soldiers were sent to rear hospitals and only 5 percent of them recuperated enough to return to fight. Psychiatrists weren't assigned to combat divisions nor were psychiatric treatment units constructed near the front.

But the military eventually began to address the problem in 1943, creating forward psychiatric care treatment areas. Two military psychiatrists, Roy R. Grinker and John P. Spiegel, had success introducing psychotherapeutic treatment for traumatized US Army Air Force airmen, giving them sodium pentothal, which induced a dream state and encouraged them to reexperience their trauma; this allowed soldiers to have more control of their stress-inducing memories.

Grinker and Spiegel argued for a far more sympathetic approach to soldiers who displayed signs of trauma, reasoning that "it would seem to be a more rational question to ask why the soldier does not succumb to anxiety, rather than why he does," they wrote in a document distributed to medical officers in 1943. The psychiatrists advocated for the idea that every man had his "breaking point," and they estimated that it would come between one hundred days and one year of combat duty. By 1945, the military was recommending forward medical stations that echoed Salmon's key principles: immediacy, proximity, expectancy, simplicity, and centrality.

In the beginning of World War II, there had been about three dozen psychiatrists working for the US armed forces. By 1945, there were more than two thousand medical officers assigned to neuropsychiatry. Grinker and Spiegel had led a new way of thinking about war trauma, but the military brass was still divided on how much to address the problem, because many officers believed that, by confronting it, the problem would become more exposed and subsequently more pervasive. (See slap-happy General Patton.) What they all agreed on was to dispose of the term *shell shock*; the medical community thought it lacked specificity and the military considered it damaging to morale. They decided that the new name for war neuroses should be either *combat fatigue* or *battle fatigue*.

After the war, veterans had a lot going for them. They had won. They were heroes. And they were rewarded with an expansive GI Bill that gave them access to higher education and mortgages. The postwar boom economy provided a multitude of opportunities. But despite World War II's reputation for releasing victorious, adaptable GIs into the postwar economy, 37 percent of discharges from the military were for mental illness or other mental problems. There had been 850,000 soldiers admitted to army hospitals for neuropsychiatric disorders. Forty percent of those admissions happened overseas and the majority back in the United States.

Despite the rosy depictions of jubilant crowds celebrating "V-J" Day in Times Square and the prospect of GIs gliding forward on a surging economy, there was a significant swath of veterans who carried with them diagnoses of serious mental health issues.

POSTWAR AMERICA ushered in a new era for mental health treatment. The United States began to address a wide range of mental health questions through expanded research and new treatment resources with the passage of the National Mental Health Act of 1946. By the mid-1950s more than 500,000 people were hospitalized in state and county mental health institutions: Visits to "the loony bin" had become part of the culture. But awareness was dawning, thanks to exposés such as Albert Deutsch's 1948 *The Shame of the States*, which exposed the overcrowded and crumbling conditions of the nation's asylums.

The expanding mental health industry moved to replace institutionalization with rehabilitation and the use of psychopharmacology, led by new drugs such as lithium salts, chlorpromazine, and imipramine, which offered treatment options for persistent and severe psychiatric symptoms.

Over the next two decades, culminating with the Community Mental Health Act of 1963, asylums and hospitals were replaced by other facilities, such as local mental health homes and outpatient services, which were becoming effective ways of treating people who were bipolar, depressed, or schizophrenic.

The Korean War, which lasted from 1950 to 1953, put the evolving field of psychology on the front lines. There was an increase in soldiers suffering from mental trauma compared to World War II, but, unfortunately, despite the severity of the conflict and the high casualty rate of 33,000 American soldiers killed, the war's impact on those who fought it has not received the same analysis as the wars that preceded and followed it. It is, after all, known as the "forgotten war," not an irrelevant factor for soldiers who came home struggling with adapting to civilian life.

To start, the Korean War was officially not considered a war and was named the Korean "conflict," which only further alienated the American soldiers who fought it. Americans entered the war supporting South Koreans against the invading North Koreans, at a time when the front lines were constantly shifting. Early on, North Korea routed the South for months. Americans who were largely inexperienced in combat were thrust into a conflict that included well-below-freezing weather conditions and extreme brutality; there were inhumane massacres of civilians meted out by both the North and the South. It is estimated that more than three million people, mostly civilians, died during the war.

At the beginning of US involvement in 1950, there was an astoundingly high rate of "neuropsychiatric casualties": 250 per 1,000 soldiers. But the military's forward psychiatry treatment efficiently returned more than 80 percent of those suffering mental issues back to the front.

Military psychiatrists began to call the mental strain on soldiers "gross stress reaction," which included symptoms such as preoccupation with the traumatic stressor, nightmares, irritability, increased tendency to startle, and hyperarousal. Military medical practitioners looked for signs and symptoms of the disorder, incurring a diagnosis rate two to three times greater than rates in previous wars.

In 1952, the American Psychiatric Association (APA) released the *Diagnostic and Statistical Manual of Mental Disorders,* or DSM-1, its first manual of mental disorders as a reference book for psychiatrists. The DSM-1 included war trauma, and referred to it as "gross stress reaction," a temporary mental disturbance caused by extreme environmental stress, often occurring in patients without a previous condition. It is notable that the disorder was diagnosed as happening to otherwise normal individuals as well as the notion that it was temporary, suggesting it would be resolved if the patient were to be removed from the stressful situation.

The diagnosis could have served to destigmatize the condition, but Korean War veterans returned to the United States having fought a war that had been censored by the military and having received little public support. The US military and veterans mostly went silent on the issue of war trauma, hoping it could be deemed a temporary condition that could be left behind on the battlefield.

Alas, one 1994 VA study compared possible PTSD in soldiers from World War II and the Korean War. Those who had never sought psychiatric treatment were marginally the same. But among those who had previously sought treatment, 43 percent more Korean War veterans than World War II veterans, for a total of 80 percent, had current PTSD. The number seems inordinately high, but the study appeared in a respected peer-reviewed journal, *Psychiatric Clinics of North America.*

Of course, the "forgotten war" would be eclipsed by the "quagmire" in Vietnam. There are perplexing questions regarding the psychological impact of that more recent conflict on the soldiers who fought it. Much has been made of one report that just 12 cases per 1,000 soldiers were treated for psychiatric issues, a far better rate than the Korean War (73 out of 1,000, which covers the entire conflict) or World War II (28 to 101 out of 1,000, depending on deployment). As few as 5 percent of Vietnam War soldiers sought psychiatric treatment in 1966.

Combing through studies—and a word of caution for this entire chapter; I would take the numbers presented here that come from a wide range of sources over a century of changing methods and standards with a grain of salt, no matter how reputable the journals and researchers may be—there is a general perception that the American soldier fared relatively better psychologically in Vietnam than in previous wars *in the early years*. This, despite only 140 psychiatrists being deployed to Vietnam.

The early success in Vietnam has been attributed to more aggressive treatment of psychiatric casualties in forward areas, the limiting of tours of duty to one year, and more frequent removal of soldiers from fighting to rest "inside the wire"—lessons learned from previous wars.

The positive results actually contributed to the removal of "gross stress reaction" from 1968's DSM-II. But as the war heated up and then dragged on, the psychiatric profile of the American soldier changed. There was a fourfold increase in soldiers needing psychiatric treatment, a trend that was exacerbated (and muddled) by the increasingly pervasive use of readily available drugs, including marijuana, hashish, and heroin.

In 1970, the US Senate Committee on Veterans' Affairs convened a hearing to examine "the psychological predicament of the Vietnam veteran," where psychiatrist Robert Jay Lifton, an anti-war activist, testified to a "psychic numbing" that soldiers were undergoing, one that didn't disappear upon returning home. Lifton brought a wealth of knowledge about the effect of trauma; after serving as an air force psychiatrist during the Korean War, he had studied the survivors of the bombing of Hiroshima, which culminated in his 1969 National Book Award–winning *Death in Life*. Lifton had developed the concept of "psychic numbing" as "the need for such a defense against otherwise overwhelming anxiety and guilt in relationship to their immersion in death."

A year later, a Vietnam veteran, Sergeant Dwight "Skip" Howard, was shot dead when he tried to rob a store in Detroit. Howard, who had been diagnosed with "depression caused by post-Vietnam adjustment problems," appeared to want to be killed by the store owner. The tragic incident preceded an essay written by psychiatrist Chaim Shatan that was published in the *New York Times* in 1972, titled "Post-Vietnam Syndrome," in which he described a disturbing psychological trend in veterans that complemented Lifton's testimony: Soldiers were fraught with guilt, confusion, rage, and alienation, and were prone to self-destructive behavior. They were unable to adapt to civilian life. Shatan reported that in response to this situation, there was an emerging movement of "group rap" sessions organized by traumatized veterans who felt ignored by the VA. He concluded that veterans' need to grieve was being stifled, leaving them in "an encapsulated, never-ending past [that] deprives the present of meaning."

The criteria for this emerging war trauma diagnosis included the concept of delayed onset: The symptoms could appear years after the wartime trauma. In 1978, Lifton and Shatan presented their findings regarding veteran case studies to the APA's Committee on Reactive Disorders and helped coin the diagnosis "post-traumatic stress disorder," which was added to the DSM-III in 1980. (There had also been a concurrent movement to address long-term traumatic symptoms in Holocaust survivors, which also influenced the 1980 DSM-III change.)

The DSM-III characterized PTSD with three major elements: reliving the memories of the traumatic experience (commonly described as "flashbacks"); avoidance of reminders of the trauma (emotional numbing, detachment); and increased arousal (hypervigilance, irritability, memory lapses, sleep disturbances, and an exaggerated startle response).

The new diagnosis gave a new name to the psychological problems that veterans had been experiencing. And it dovetailed with a new popular perception of the Vietnam soldier as trauma-tized, especially on the big screen. After disturbing, nuanced films of the 1970s, such as *Taxi Driver*, *The Deer Hunter*, *Apocalypse Now*, and *Coming Home*, steeped audiences in the unhappy lives of veteran anti-heroes, the 1980s were punctuated with Vietnam vets who could kick ass but were equally haunted, in films such as *First Blood* and *Missing in Action* (and their numerous sequels). At the same time, on a higher level of discourse, Vietnam veteran authors, such as Tim O'Brien, Philip Caputo, Robert Stone, and Larry Heinemann, were publishing books, giving voice to Viet-nam veterans wrestling with their war experiences.

The trauma that the veterans carried after Vietnam also found physical form in the conditions of soldiers exposed to Agent Orange, the toxic herbicide that the US used to defoliate the jungles in order to expose enemy Viet Cong. Veterans reported higher rates of cancer, birth defects, and other conditions that led to a $180 million out-of-court settlement with the chemical companies responsible for the herbicide. The case was a peren-nial news item. In the late 1980s and early 1990s, 52,000 veterans or their families received payments. An additional $74 million was distributed to social service organizations that worked with 239,000 Vietnam veterans and their families.

At the same time, Congress was bolstering the response to the psychiatric needs of Vietnam veterans. The Veterans' Health Programs Extension and Improvement Act of 1979 opened the appointment process for psychiatrists to work in higher-ranking positions within the VA. And then the Veterans' Health Care Amendments Act of 1983 and the Veterans' Health Care Act of 1984 provided psychiatric counseling to all veterans, as well as developing special PTSD treatment and research programs.

By the mid-1980s, hundreds of thousands of veterans were getting treatment. Surveys showed that between 15 and 30 percent of Vietnam War veterans had PTSD, or had had it in the past.

It is worth noting that more than a decade after the diagnosis was established, World War II veterans weren't being treated for PTSD by the VA. "PTSD was a code word for Vietnam Stress Syndrome," Duke University professor Harold Kudler says. But by the mid-1990s, an ex-POW program at the VA and Vet Centers began to recognize older veterans with PTSD. The notion that war trauma could apply to all soldiers in any war was beginning to take root.

IN 1980, after the Iran hostage crisis and the Russian invasion of Afghanistan, President Jimmy Carter declared that the United States would defend oil interests in the Persian Gulf, known as the Carter Doctrine, launching a militarization of the area that lasts to today. Over the next four decades, our combat troops have been dedicated to a series of wars and engagements that have resulted in a new population of veterans with PTSD.

Our first war during this period, the Persian Gulf War of 1990 and 1991, was largely an aerial war to repel Iraq out of Kuwait, which it had invaded. In addition to an onslaught of artillery, the US Air Force launched more than 100,000 sorties and dropped more than 88,500 tons of bombs. With 425,000 troops deployed, the ground war lasted just one hundred hours.

Despite the relative ease with which the United States executed the war—there were 383 US casualties compared to thousands of Iraqis killed—a disturbing wave of soldiers reported a number of symptoms that was dubbed "Gulf War syndrome," a combination of headache, insomnia, joint pain, problems with memory and breathing, cognitive impairment, fatigue, intestinal issues, and skin abnormalities. As many as 250,000, more than 30 percent of the 700,000 troops that ultimately served during the engagement, reported symptoms.

A 2014 VA report listed the following *inconclusive* causes of Gulf War syndrome: chemical, pharmaceutical, and other environmental exposures, depleted uranium, pesticides, oil well fires, and receipt of multiple vaccines. In the same report, the VA indicated that fewer than 10 percent of Gulf War veterans had PTSD, which it considers clinically distinct from Gulf War syndrome.

And then, on September 11, 2001, the Al-Qaeda terrorist attacks on US soil initiated our current era of "endless wars" in the Middle East. The conflicts in Afghanistan and Iraq have resulted in close to seven thousand American casualties. The enemy's most effective weapons, suicide bombers and improvised explosive devices (IEDs), which have caused more than half of the US deaths, have had a distinctly menacing effect on the minds of soldiers, in a way reminiscent of the impact of the Viet Cong's unpredictable guerrilla warfare on US soldiers in Vietnam. Both engagements were also seemingly without end and were questioned back home because of mistrust of government motives and ambiguous results. There are also differences, the first being that in the twenty-first century, the United States has had an all-volunteer army. Another is that there is now an institutional and mainstream awareness that war can have a debilitating, long-term traumatic effect on soldiers' minds.

According to a VA report, the early psychological impact of combat in Afghanistan and Iraq may have been troubling but wasn't overwhelming; 15 percent of veterans who enrolled for health services in early 2004 received mental health–related diagnoses after one year. But by 2008, that number nearly doubled to 28 percent. That same year, a much-cited report by the RAND Corporation estimated that 26 percent of returning troops had mental health issues, primarily PTSD, depression, and generalized anxiety.

The VA report's principal author attributed the rise to repeat deployments, the particularly perilous nature of combat in the region, the lack of troop morale, the diminishing support for the wars back home, and the growing awareness of PTSD. Advances in medical technology also meant more soldiers who would have otherwise died were alive, albeit with severe bodily or mental injuries. Exacerbating the cases was the nature of IED-related injuries, particularly traumatic brain injury (TBI), which can produce PTSD-like symptoms. It was predicted that in addition to the thousands of soldiers who suffered direct head wounds, hundreds of thousands of troops could have suffered mild TBI because of nearby IED blast waves.

With more than two million Americans having been deployed to Iraq and Afghanistan, the studies suggest that there could be more than 500,000 mentally wounded American veterans. No matter that approximately 10 percent of soldiers were actually involved in combat; PTSD has been known to affect soldiers in rear positions more often than those actually on the front lines.

A series of reports began to paint a portrait of a new generation of traumatized soldiers. In 2008, the New York Times reported that there had been 121 recent veterans who either had killed someone or had been accused of killing someone after returning to the United States. According to the VA, in 2018, veterans accounted for 13.8 percent of all deaths by suicide among US adults but constituted only 8 percent of the same population.

One study showed that quick turnarounds between deployments or deploying too early raised the risk of death by suicide. And of the suicides in 2017, 59 percent had a recently diagnosed mental health or substance use disorder.

The military had tried to prevent the damaging impact of deployment. In 1999, the Department of Defense had directed all services to implement combat stress control programs that would prevent, identify, and treat psychological trauma before, during, and after deployments.

By 2007, the navy and Marines Corps convened officers, chaplains, and medical and mental health professionals to create the Marine Corps' Combat Operational Stress Control (COSC) program, which emphasized strengthening soldiers through training, unit cohesion, and model leadership. The program also sought to mitigate stressors, like encouraging proper sleep and constructively discussing potentially traumatizing experiences in the field. It directed officers to better understand the psychological status of each soldier in a unit. And it instructed for the employment of medical or psychiatric treatment for soldiers displaying signs of stress.

A similar approach was applied by the army, where, by 2008, soldiers received so-called Battlemind training before being deployed. Previously, the army only ran postdeployment health briefings. But Battlemind was supposed to be a fully integrative training program before, during, and after deployment. Battlemind is an acronym that stands for Buddies (connecting with fellow soldiers rather than withdrawing), Accountability, Targeted aggression (as opposed to inappropriate aggression),

Tactical awareness (as opposed to hypervigilance), Lethally armed (responsible wielding of weaponry), Emotional control (as opposed to anger or detachment), Mission operational security (rather than secretiveness), Individual responsibility (versus guilt), Nondefensive driving (but not aggressive driving), and Discipline (not conflict).

The program was instituted to instill strength to help soldiers face fears and the adversity of combat. It included rudimentary lessons, such as being explicit about what the reality of combat and deployment would be like. Psychological debriefings were given in theater and upon redeployment and postdeployment for partners and family to help with the transition back to civilian life. This last element was crucial, because the Battlemind program was directed toward the soldier in combat, which is not how he or she would be expected to behave after deployment. As one of the manuals says, "Battlemind may be 'hazardous' to your social & behavioral health in the home zone."

"There was a lot of wisdom to Battlemind," says Dr. Harold Kudler. "Did it work? I don't think there's a lot of evidence. But it was the right thing to do."

Dr. Kudler says that the army has scrubbed Battlemind from its training programs and websites in its ever-evolving series of attempts to combat PTSD. He says that there are no completely effective ways to prevent PTSD. "Maybe you can improve a person's resilience but you can't make someone bulletproof," he says. "If you could, I'd be concerned about those soldiers."

IN 2021, with only a few thousand soldiers stationed in Iraq and Afghanistan (whereas, at its peak, there were 270,000 troops deployed a decade earlier), the endless wars are nearing some sort of an end. But for many of the soldiers who return home, there is this terrible legacy that they carry. More than a third of the nearly three million soldiers who served in those engagements have applied for disability. And about a third of those treated have been diagnosed with PTSD.

The proportion of soldiers who claim mental disabilities has increased with each war since World War II at the same time that the number who experience combat has decreased. For instance, the first Gulf War—a very limited engagement—produced nearly twice the disability rate of World War II.

But war trauma does not happen in a vacuum. It is related to historical and cultural shifts. And that includes structural changes. In 2010, the VA decided to allow veterans to claim PTSD as a disability without having to cite a particular incident—a verifiable IED attack, for instance—and instead could just report being impaired. Now the VA is treating over a million veterans with PTSD.

Today, PTSD has a dominant presence at the VA. It is supported by the institutional system and accepted by a generation that has become accustomed to the benefits and ease with which one can claim it, which, in turn, breeds doubt about it. It's confusing. The widespread acknowledgment of PTSD also endows it with insecurity; the question as to whether or not it's legitimate is its constant shadow.

Slaughterhouse-Five was published at a critical juncture in the evolution of war trauma in America, representing its past, portraying its present, and anticipating its future. Billy Pilgrim is a quintessential example of the "psychic numbing" that Robert Jay Lifton presented to the US Senate in 1970. Lifton, who contributed greatly to the development of the PTSD diagnosis, once wrote that "psychic numbing" also applies to "everyone who performs some kind of useful function—medical, artistic, or investigative—while confronting death." Sounds like Vonnegut. Lifton agrees with me that Vonnegut struggled with the same subject as he did, but creatively. He calls him a "kindred spirit."

I spoke with the 94-year-old psychiatrist, who went to Cornell at the same time as Vonnegut and who knew the author casually in New York City in their later years. Lifton told me that he was once surprised to receive a call in the middle of the night in the late 1970s, or perhaps it was the early 1980s, from Vonnegut. Lifton had recently given an interview on television regarding the psychic numbing of trauma survivors, and Vonnegut called him out of the blue to express his appreciation for what Lifton had said. "He didn't talk in a conventional way but he emitted ideas tangentially," Lifton says. "It was clear that he wanted to check in and give his approval."

Lifton says that he had read *Slaughterhouse-Five* soon after it came out in 1969. "I admired it enormously. I thought it was one of the great novels of that time," he says. "It had so much to say obliquely and indirectly about trauma and massive killing, and that sort of subject is very difficult to write about. His method was this oblique exploration of unreality which nonetheless is a source of truth.

"The survivor and the psychology of the survivor have been a lifelong preoccupation of mine," Lifton adds. "Vonnegut's writing fit particularly well into issues that I was struggling with."

In 1973, Lifton wrote an essay titled "Survivor as Creator," in which he analyzed the literature of survival by authors such as Albert Camus, Günter Grass, and Vonnegut.

He wrote of Vonnegut as a seer, a survivor of his World War II experiences who had seen the worst of death and who returned "to make sense—or anti-sense—of a world dominated by every variety of holocaust and every variety of numbing."

"His hard-won 'knowledge' of death that both defines and plagues him, tends to be fragmentary at best and half-articulate yet that knowledge is precious in the extreme," Lifton wrote. "It takes shape from the survivor's struggle to grasp his experience and render it significant, his struggle to formulate his death immersion. Only by coming to such knowledge can the survivor cease to be immobilized by his death imprint, his death guilt, and his psychic numbing."

In response to my query, Lifton says it's "too simplistic" to say that Vonnegut's book influenced him or the eventual addition of PTSD to the DSM. But he adds, "With the Vietnam War, there was a preoccupation with death and trauma. And Vonnegut's book, although it was about Dresden, it contributed to that societal preoccupation and gave a particular emphasis to how to approach it creatively with the imaginative expression of mockery. He didn't create that atmosphere. He contributed to it."

I would argue that Lifton undervalues Vonnegut's contribution, but it is not surprising considering he downplays his own. I agree that it may be simplifying to look at it as cause and effect, but *Slaughterhouse-Five* articulates much of what we call PTSD today—and that includes both the diagnosis and the doubts sown into it.

CHAPTER NINE

A PTSD PRIMER AND AN INFINITE JESTER

IN APRIL 2019, singer Ariana Grande posted brain scans of a "healthy brain," a "PTSD" brain, and her own brain on Instagram for her 200 million followers. It wasn't very scientific but she intended to show how damaged hers was. Her brain appeared to have much more activity than the others. Two years prior, a suicide bomber killed twenty-two people at her concert in Manchester, England, and the singer had been struggling with the trauma. "Not a joke," she wrote.

Whether it was a high or low point in PTSD awareness is open to interpretation, but it was yet another demonstration of how the diagnosis pervades the culture, albeit as a contentious issue. It has been applied to sexual assault survivors, victims of child abuse, survivors of school shootings, and many other forms of trauma, including collective events, such as the September 11 attacks and the COVID-19 pandemic. Regarding the Al-Qaeda attacks in 2001, a RAND Corporation survey concluded that 44 percent of Americans had "substantial symptoms of stress" because of 9/11.

Before we get into defining what PTSD is, which is necessary if we're going to look at whether or not Billy Pilgrim and Kurt Vonnegut had it, I want to briefly address the skepticism about it. When a brain scan can win sympathy and a medical diagnosis can mean a monthly cash disability payment, there's inevitably going to be wariness that PTSD claims are being made for ulterior motives. The VA determines a soldier's disability check by rating the percentage by which he or she is disabled. For a veteran without a spouse or any dependents, a 10 percent disability rating generates a $142.29 monthly payment. A 70 percent rating brings a $1,426.17 payment. A 100 percent rating means he or she can receive $3,106.04 per month.

In addition to the VA disability payments, there are other potential motivations to pretend to have PTSD. They include reducing criminal liability, seeking financial gain in a civil dispute, receiving priority treatment by the VA, and obtaining shelter or medical care from other sources.

A 2007 *American Journal of Public Health* study indicated that after veterans with a lower disability rating went to a high rating, their use of mental health services decreased, a trend its authors called "troubling."

But most studies indicate malingering occurs in a slim minority of cases. Dr. Kudler says that in his experience "there are very, very few" veterans who malinger. "In fact, it is likely that most veterans who actually have PTSD would rather not tell anyone about it," he says, adding that cases in which a veteran is caught lying about having PTSD tend to be overreported.

PTSD very much exists. Real traumas happen to real people who have real wounds that can indeed be picked up by hormonal system blood testing and brain scan technology that allows researchers to observe changes in the volume, structure, and blood flow in the brain. For example, the hippocampus, which is vital to memory and context processing, has been shown to be reduced in volume in those who suffer trauma. And changes in the amygdala, which can also be caused by trauma, can distort the fear response.

The VA has aggressively supported such research, and also has its own National Posttraumatic Stress Disorder Brain Bank, a "brain tissue biodepository" with the brains of deceased people who had PTSD or other major depressive disorders. The bank has been used for testing, including one Boston VA study published in 2020 in which older adults with PTSD showed accelerated aging in brain tissue related to their having a variant of a particular gene.

But however revealing such research can be, a person's brain scan, or "brain thingy," as Grande later described it, or blood levels can't be used to diagnose PTSD. For that, a patient must present symptoms to a clinician who deduces the diagnosis as defined by criteria established by the American Psychiatric Association. The APA's latest revision of the DSM, the DSM-5 of 2013, categorizes PTSD as a trauma- and stressor-related disorder rather than an anxiety disorder. And it identifies the trigger to PTSD as "exposure to actual or threatened death, serious injury or sexual violation."

According to the DSM-5, the exposure must result from at least one of the following events: directly experiencing trauma; witnessing a traumatic event in person; learning that the traumatic event occurred to a close family member or close friend; or experiencing firsthand repeated or extreme exposure to aversive details of the traumatic event. And the disturbance must cause "clinically significant distress or impairment in the individual's social interactions, capacity to work or other important areas of functioning."

The VA determines that a soldier has PTSD if he or she is reliving the experience (flashback), avoiding the event, having negative thoughts (depression, numbness), experiencing hyperarousal (feeling on edge or rage, both of which can lead to drug or alcohol abuse), or having troubled sleep several weeks or months after the incident. Additional symptoms can include social withdrawal, loss of memory about the event, and distorted sense of blame of self or others. More than previous DSMs, the current criteria in DSM-5 account for the "fight," not just "flight," reaction.

More than 50 percent of Americans have experienced a traumatic event, and, of those, 10 percent of men experience PTSD, while 20 percent of women do, according to the military. Events like combat and sexual assault are more likely to cause PTSD, but there is no clear determination of what kind of person will develop PTSD, although research indicates that soldiers who have inherited mental disorders or have had abusive or otherwise traumatic childhoods are predisposed to the condition.

It is uncanny how closely Billy Pilgrim's time travel, mental dysfunction, and social withdrawal mirror the PTSD diagnosis. To plumb this connection, I reached out to a number of vets who expressed an affinity for Vonnegut, including Matt Gallagher, a former army captain deployed in Iraq, who wrote a memoir, *Kaboom: Embracing the Suck in a Savage Little War*, and a war-based fiction novel, *Youngblood*. Gallagher, who originally comes from Reno, Nevada, has taught a veterans' writing workshop called Words After War, which was launched in 2013 as part of a nonprofit organization, Iraq and Afghanistan Veterans of

America. He and I met at the Ontario bar in Williamsburg midway between where we each live in Brooklyn.

Gallagher, who is laid-back and cheerful in a way that makes New Yorkers like me feel a little nervous, had written an essay in which he praised Vonnegut's writing and described himself as "unstuck" at times, a metaphor he used for being displaced between his war engagement and his postwar life. But he also wrote that he felt that he was one of the "lucky ones." And, over beer, delighted to have a newborn son and newlywed wife waiting for him at home, Gallagher affably described himself as no longer "unstuck."

Gallagher suggested I talk with Matthew Mellina, another Iraq War veteran and member of the writing workshop. When Mellina was told about my book, he told Gallagher, "Vonnegut is God." Over the next months, I spent many hours with Mellina on the phone and at his home in Long Island and drinking in bars. We also met up with Gallagher, other veteran-writers, and their sort-of mentor, *New York Times* editor Peter Catapano, for a lively dinner at a Polish restaurant in the East Village, where Mellina remained mostly silent, occasionally stepping out for a smoke.

"I think he's a very good writer," Catapano later said of Mellina. "But he's too critical of himself."

It took time, but with Mellina's interest and openness I was able to put together the pieces of his story.

WHEN MELLINA LEFT THE MILITARY IN 2007, he was diagnosed with PTSD at a 30 percent rating. Twelve years later, Mellina is at a 100 percent rating, thanks to the PTSD, TBI (traumatic brain injury), and a series of surgeries he's been getting for his back and neck.

At the age of thirty-six, Mellina now lives in his parents' home in Ronkonkoma, New York, the last train station on the Long Island Railroad. Mellina half-jokingly calls himself "retired." He hasn't been able to hold down a job. He has tried working on a screenplay and early on wrote a few essays, two of which were published on the *New York Times* website, and wants to write more, but the words haven't come easily.

"I am going to be completely candid. I've been catatonic for ten years," he says while sitting in the living room in his father's armchair with a pack of Newports at his side. "I have barely done anything with my life. I have run from everything by standing very still," a concept he has borrowed from a David Foster Wallace short story, "Forever Overhead," about bees—that they have to move very fast to stay afloat.

For years, Mellina has been getting regular surgeries on his back and neck, for "living hard, fast and as destructive as possible," he says, and a life of "abusing the crap out of myself," which included enlisting in the military and being involved in several rollovers, experiencing a few IED attacks, and carrying a large squad automatic weapon, also known as a SAW machine gun, around Iraq, where he served one tour in 2006. "I definitely had my ass handed to me," he says of his deployment.

Mellina does and doesn't agree with his PTSD diagnosis. "I am not the poster child for PTSD," he says. "I don't have the battle flashbacks. I don't suffer from it as others do."

Mellina occasionally halts himself in mid-thought, pulling at his substantial beard. He takes off his baseball cap and rubs his bald head. He gets frustrated when he thinks he's not being articulate, which is rare. He's more well-spoken than most of us. But it's true that, on the subject of PTSD, he gets muddled.

"I don't believe soldiers get PTSD," he says. "It is supposedly caused by a singular moment, a raping, a beating, sudden death. With soldiers, we are already prepared for that: the shock and awe of combat. We have been inoculated against it."

Mellina spends most of his time reading, playing video games, sleeping, and just thinking himself into spirals. "My biggest struggle is boredom," he says. "It's my Achilles' heel. It's what's probably most dragged down my life since returning home. Complete and utter boredom. Nothing will ever top what you did. You can never get that kind of experience again, or those endorphins back."

With shame and pride, Mellina recalls lethal chicken fights on cement with his combat brothers, naked wrestling matches, popping off guns in burnt-out warehouses, and locker room behavior like a guy wrapping his penis around his wrist and then making a buddy look at what time it is.

"We were kids. We all came in and transitioned into something different," he says. "I wouldn't call us adults—more like raving lunatics."

Mellina enlisted in the army in the elite explosive ordnance disposal unit, hoping to do something that meant something. And then, he says, he hoped to not come back. He already had a "dismal" opinion of the world and "went to the war to find out if I was right or wrong about everything," he says. "I came back to the civilian world and didn't have a clue what I was doing. You feel grown up and changed and you come back to this mess."

The "mess" he refers to is everyday life: family, a job, trying to find a girlfriend. Mellina didn't know what to make of it all, and he didn't want help from the VA. "I wasn't into getting help when I first got out. I know I am fucked," he says.

Matthew Mellina on "burn duty," disposing of American soldiers' feces in
northern Baghdad, Iraq, in 2006. Courtesy of Matthew Mellina.

About five years after returning, he began to see a therapist. "The reason I joined therapy was to prevent my loved ones
from worrying too much. It was never about getting me straight.
I know I am crooked," he says. Mellina has a son with an ex-
girlfriend, and after trying to maintain a relationship with him

Mellina hasn't seen him in two years. Mellina doesn't feel like he can be a father. "I didn't want my shit to be transferred over to him," he says.

What exactly is his problem? Mellina says that he has a bad temper. Even before the war, he was obsessive-compulsive and would have nightmares. "War amplified who I already was," he says. "I was always a little nutty. When I was in the military and the war, it multiplied all the bad habits, every quirk that you could call a mental disorder."

Mellina finds reading to be his greatest ballast. And he has turned to *Slaughterhouse-Five*, which first "gob-smacked" him when he was sixteen. He read it again before his deployment and again after he came home. "We are very similar," he says of Billy Pilgrim. "I was so out of my element. I had no clue what I was doing. He's me. I have always felt out of place, especially with the men I served. It was always weird. I am more comfortable in my skin when I am reading something like *Slaughterhouse*."

Mellina identifies more with the postwar Billy Pilgrim, the old-man Billy Pilgrim, than the one who experiences war. "Billy is bored. He is bored to the point that it is detrimental to his mental and physical health," he says.

When he finally spoke with a therapist, Mellina couldn't suss out what was just his way of thinking, if he was depressed, or if he had PTSD. He does have clearly identifiable PTSD symptoms: He gets anxious when he goes outside or if his back isn't against a wall, and he has had trouble concentrating while driving. He is constantly on edge. And he gets nauseated by certain smells, such as beef stew, which he ate too often when he was outside the wire because those were the only MREs (meals ready-to-eat) left over. In general, he says, he "thinks too vividly at times."

Still, he believes that the trauma he lives with isn't rooted in what he experienced during the war but what happened when he got home. It's like he wants to drop the *P* and the *D* off of his diagnosis; he lives with the traumatizing stress of everyday life.

Mellina stopped going to therapy more than a year ago, but he takes an antidepressant and an antianxiety drug that also dulls his chronic physical pain.

"When I talk about my PTSD, I am not in denial about it. I was already fucked up about the world," he says. "In cognitive behavioral therapy [one of the primary psychological methods the military uses for PTSD], you go over one event over and over again. You speak about it. Every day, you tell the story over and over again. Getting it out is supposed to relieve you of it being inside you. They make you pick one event. There's no fucking way. 'It's not one singular event,' I tell them. 'Could I have dozens of events?'"

In the basement of his parents' house, Mellina sleeps with one of his metal army ammunition boxes under his bed. It's about the size of a toaster oven and full of memorabilia: pictures of a dead buddy, Justin Jarrett; a piece of the IED that killed him; an Iraqi torture device that went up the nose and into the brain; and a piece of glass from the destroyed World Trade Center. These are not cheerful mementos; they're traumatic pieces of memory that he sleeps over every night.

It reminds me of something that Dr. Kudler refers to, which Freud wrote in his 1939 book, *Moses and Monotheism*. "He noted that trauma survivors paradoxically both over-remember and avoid their traumatic history," Dr. Kudler says. "We don't know what to do with these memories—they don't fit the psychological system we want to have, so we keep coming back to them even as we keep trying to bury them until we find a way to accommodate them and/or transcend them through a new psychic structure. When this goes well, it's now called 'post-traumatic growth,' but I don't like trying to make a silk purse out of a sow's ear."

I ask Dr. Kudler in general terms about a veteran, such as Mellina, who is frustrated by his treatment. "Different people connect to different therapies," he says. "Virtually every therapy for psychological trauma is based on the idea that trauma prevents you from processing memory. They all have this common idea that, if you do this, you'll finally be able to process/metabolize/digest/integrate that experience."

The list of VA treatments for PTSD is long—it includes quality of life changes, meditation, service dogs, medical marijuana, and medications such as Zoloft and Prozac—but there are three primary therapies that have been most successful: cognitive processing therapy, prolonged exposure therapy, and eye movement desensitization and reprocessing.

Cognitive processing therapy (CPT) is a form of cognitive behavioral treatment that was developed in the 1980s to help survivors of sexual trauma. It involves changing thinking patterns through twelve sessions. "Think of it as asbestos gloves for the psyche which enable you to begin to contain and manage traumatic memories and their related thoughts and feelings," Dr. Kudler says.

There are two primary "stuck" points, according to the VA's application of CPT: assimilation and over-accommodation. For the former, a person's trauma is detrimentally assimilated into his or her belief system. So, for example, the belief that good things happen to good people and bad things happen to bad people means that the patient must be bad if something bad happened to him or her. With over-accommodation, the person with PTSD exaggerates his or her belief system, such as believing all humans are evil if he or she is exposed to an evil act by one person. Correcting those stuck points tends to be the goal of CPT.

The purpose of prolonged exposure therapy is to make memories of traumatic events less fearful. In what's called imaginal exposure, a patient talks about his or her trauma with a therapist and then listens to recordings of that trauma narrative between sessions in the hope that the veteran eventually attains a sense of control of the disturbing memories. And "in vivo" exposure involves repeated actual, physical engagement of situations and activities related to the trauma. Both are implemented with the goal of increasing a sense of mastery of the veteran's memories and ability to function.

In eye movement desensitization and reprocessing, or EMDR, the veteran thinks or talks about traumatic memories while focusing on stimuli like eye movements, hand taps, and sounds. EMDR is based on the theory of adaptive information processing, which holds that people process experiences by connecting them with related emotions and memories. PTSD occurs when an experience is improperly processed and stored dysfunctionally. By calling up a trauma while focusing on alternating tones or a therapist's finger taps, the memory is assimilated in the brain differently. Even the VA says it's unclear why it works, but it remains one of its most effective treatments.

According to the VA's National Center for PTSD, 53 percent of patients who receive one of these three therapies are cured, a number that Dr. Kudler is skeptical of. He suggests that success rate may not account for the veterans who drop out of the treatments. He adds that any "cure" has to be viewed in context.

"Therapy doesn't change the past," he says, but, also as important, "I've never met a patient who couldn't make progress."

MELLINA KEEPS THE EULOGY he wrote and read for Justin Jarrett in the ammunition box he keeps under his bed. Along with Jarrett, three other American soldiers, James Ellis, Raymond Armijo, and Kristofer Walker, were also killed when a bomb exploded near their humvee on October 2, 2006.

Minutes before the attack, Mellina was on the radio with Jarrett, bullshitting with him, waiting for him to return to base. What led to Jarrett's death is a confusing narrative that still swirls in Mellina's head; he is still trying to set it straight.

It appears to begin about six months earlier, when Captain Ian Weikel, a beloved 31-year-old leader of the 710 Cavalry, was killed in an IED attack. "After that, we went nuts," says Mellina, who wasn't yet "in country" but had trained with Weikel. Mellina says his platoon, also known as "the Hooligans," was part of a high-pressure campaign seeking vengeance for Weikel's death. "We were ruthless," he says. They made "unnecessary" kills, making raids to the point that the enemy heightened retaliations. Mellina alludes to possible war crimes.

In September, part of his platoon was ambushed when they entered the town of Al-Falahat, west of Fallujah, where local Shiite and Sunni militias had been fighting each other. It seems the rival Iraqi factions hated Americans more than they hated each other. Both sides began shooting at the Americans. As the platoon fought to extricate itself, Mellina and Jarrett were pinned in a corridor between buildings and an open field.

Mellina was leaning against a wall, firing his machine gun in one direction, while Jarrett faced several men about thirty yards away running toward them across the field. Jarrett pulled the trigger on his M203 single-shot grenade launcher and obliterated the insurgents' lower bodies. Suddenly, they went from being tall to being shorter. It was funny to think of it that way; that's what stuck in Jarrett's head, so that's how he told the story afterward, like their bottom halves had been chopped off. It was the first time Jarrett had killed the enemy.

The town was buzzing with insurgents and Mellina's platoon decided to detain several men and pull back to their base. As their vehicles began to leave, a detainee freed himself and jumped on Mellina's sergeant. The Iraqi wrestled the sergeant's gun from him and fired it in his face, but the safety was on, so Mellina had time to knock him down with the barrel of his shotgun. The insurgent began to run and Mellina shot him in the back, but he didn't go down. Mellina chased after him through an alley but was met with a volley of gunfire, so he returned to his vehicle.

With about six detainees rounded up in the back of an Iraqi police Toyota pickup truck, the rest of Mellina's platoon was ahead of him. Mellina drove to catch up in the rear vehicle on a dusty road when, about a hundred yards away, he saw yet another detainee in the back of the truck free himself of his zip-tie hand-cuffs and grab an Iraqi policeman's AK-47. He began shooting. It's a blur in Mellina's mind but he says there may have also been shooting coming from one of the American humvees after the prisoner grabbed the weapon.

When the shooting stopped, all of the detainees and two policemen were dead—a pile of butchered bodies in the back of the truck. The vehicles started up again and raced toward nearby Patrol Base South, an old textile factory north of Baghdad. Safely back at camp, the Americans disembarked and Mellina volunteered to clean out the truck. He wanted to do it, he says. He's not sure why.

Mellina looked at the bodies; the faces of some of the dead men had separated from their skulls. He helped carry them out and then he took a water hose and sprayed the bed of the truck to clean out the blood and flesh. It almost seemed like a normal thing to do, like washing his car back home. He sprayed water into the corners of the truck bed so that the blood was pushed out by the strong current of water onto the dry desert floor.

Jarrett sat on the ground near the truck with his head in his hands. He was crying, sobbing, and letting his emotions spill out. Despite the swirl of blood, dirt, tears, sweat, and water around him, Mellina felt relaxed and in control. The mad rush of endorphins coursing through his body began to settle.

He walked over to Jarrett and rubbed his bald head. He gave him a cigarette, "to let him know I was there," Mellina says. "I was already hardened against it. I wanted him to know that I understood." He sat next to Jarrett and didn't say anything.

Within two weeks, his best friend was killed by the IED. When Mellina called his own parents to tell them about Jarrett, his mother expressed relief that her son wasn't the one who had been killed. Mellina's then girlfriend echoed the same sentiment. Their responses bore a hole into Mellina, one that he says he still cannot fill. He could rationally understand their feeling, but he couldn't reconcile himself with it. "That changed something in me," he says.

Mellina recognizes that he has survivor's guilt, which is a significant symptom of PTSD. (And yet, the issue of guilt has been diminished in the DSM because of concern that sexual assault defendants would be asked if they felt guilty in court, which could then be used against them.) The fact that Jarrett had a wife and two children waiting for him at home, while Mellina figures his own life is worthless, makes it unbearable for him. And he broods on how, after the death of Weikel, his platoon's actions led to the killing of Jarrett. "We all knew that what we were doing was causing more harm regardless of who we killed or pressured. It only began to affect me when I realized that what we had done had precipitated everything," Mellina says. "It didn't affect me at all until later."

Without a job, Mellina has been helping his former lieutenant with nonprofit work. He has been doing some writing; he is working on a series of stories based on the military's Battlemind training program. The writing is hard.

He has promise. His *New York Times* essays are both lyrical and direct. "Don't ask me where I was at the beginning or end of Iraq. But it must have been a bar. I must have had too much to drink. I must have puffed up to some hipster while he ran his mouth, though I can't say any of this with certainty. What I can tell you is that I'm still stumbling, though I barely drink anymore," he writes.

Mellina prefers to do research. He gets high a lot. And, mostly, he reads. Reading Vonnegut has helped him navigate some of his experiences, especially the concept of being "unstuck in time." "I knew everything that was going to happen in combat was going to happen. This is where it gets really confusing and into weird territory for me," he says.

Mellina has taken the Tralfamadorian concept of time beyond the pages of *Slaughterhouse-Five*. He has done deep dives into Friedrich Nietzsche's concept of the eternal return and followed threads to the World War I poets, the writing of David Foster Wallace, and beyond.

"The eternal return states that if time and space are infinite and the matter within it is finite, then the matter will happen infinitely," he says while sinking deeper into his chair. "This means we will be back in this moment time and time again."

He does not think of the concept as a thought exercise. It is real. About five years ago, he got the word *unstuck* and an ornate timepiece tattooed on his large upper left arm. There are times when Mellina is so deep in his head that he feels that he is no longer in the present. He says that he can picture every moment in his past and play it back. He even believes he can see into the future—in a way. "It's a prediction. Of course, there are always variables and chaos," he says. "I can sit here and be in a conversation with you but my head is in a completely other time and place to the point that I am not really seeing you. It can be misread as flashbacks and unwanted memories, which are symptoms of PTSD, but I have dealt with this long before I was in the military. It's lonely. I can picture every moment in my head and play it back. It's absurdity. It's frustrating."

What's happening in his head is more interesting to him than what's happening around him. "It takes concentration to see everything that is happening around you," Mellina says. "I think that that is what Vonnegut was tapping into: the ability to see everything."

A lot of what Mellina says about time doesn't make sense to me. Plus, the fact that he smokes a lot of dope allows me to default to thinking this is circular stoner talk. The concept of time spreading out like the Rocky Mountains rather than stacked sequentially has an airy, interesting levity when you're high or if it's relayed by aliens from Tralfamadore. But in the sober, real world, it sounds pretty kooky. And yet, I genuinely believe that Mellina is experiencing time in a way that is different from me.

"Trauma destroys the fabric of time," writes David J. Morris, a veteran and journalist, in 2015's *The Evil Hours: A Biography of Post-Traumatic Stress Disorder.* "In normal time, you move from one moment to the next, sunrise to sunset, birth to death. After trauma, you may move in circles, find yourself being sucked backwards into an eddy, or bouncing about like a rubber ball from now to then and back again. August is June, June is December. What time is it? Guess again. . . . Another odd feature of traumatic time is that it doesn't just destroy the flow of the present into the future, it corrodes everything that came before, eating at moments and people from your previous life, until you can't remember why any of them mattered."

In its most literal form, the collapsing of time for a person who has PTSD is the flashback; the memory of a trauma is reexperienced as if it is actually happening all over again.

Mellina has thought his trauma into knots—a valiant effort to keep the wolves at bay but one that is fraught. I say this knowing that Vonnegut himself successfully thought his way through his war memories by writing *Slaughterhouse-Five.* But we can't all be Vonnegut. And, anyway, it's not as if he became a blissed-out Buddha after he completed the book.

Still, Mellina believes he's connected to the author in a special, almost cosmic way that he has difficulty explaining. He mentions how both he and Vonnegut cleaned up massacred bodies. He asks, "Did I become a writer because I was into him or it's how I naturally am?"

When he encountered death during his tour of duty, Mellina liked to say, "So it goes." He tells me that death and dead bodies never really had an impact on him anyway, being from a big Italian family and having gone to so many open-casket funerals for relatives. "This is going to sound weird, but I look at it like the way the Tralfamadorians do. It's just another way to look at a person."

Tim O'Brien often says that veterans should live with war trauma. Not that he wants anyone to have trauma, but as long as there are wars, then those who fight them should carry that burden. "You shouldn't recover. You should remember the nastiness of war," he says. "That's a good thing."

It is better than denying it. Or, worse, enjoying it. "There are all kinds of reactions to trauma," O'Brien says. "Including, 'I liked the pain. I liked killing.' Many of my fellow veterans tend that way." He is most disturbed by the veterans who lack empathy for their enemies in war. "It's the absence of sympathy that I find evil," he says.

"Posttraumatic syndrome is the opposite of nuts. It is what makes us human," he says. "Chipmunks don't have post-traumatic syndrome. Squirrels don't. Nor wolverines."

O'Brien believes that he had PTSD but that he no longer does. "I don't think I have it," he says with a soft chuckle. "Maybe I do, but I don't know that I do. I'll put it that way." He still has terrible dreams sometimes or drifts off in thought and gets glassy-eyed at the dinner table.

"I've used it," he says. "I've used the pain for good stuff, trying to write books and trying to teach my children to think about other people and not just themselves."

Part of his PTSD has been his inability to speak about it. "I'd write about it. But I didn't talk about it, unless I was being paid to

Immediately after graduating from Macalester College in 1968,
22-year-old Tim O'Brien was drafted into the army
and served in Vietnam. Courtesy of Tim O'Brien.

give a speech," he says. "But even then, I would never say, 'I have post-traumatic stress syndrome.' I would say, 'I have difficulty talking about it.'"

He couldn't talk with his sons about it. "I can't think of where to start, and what story to tell them," he says. "As you start to form words, they feel inadequate. They feel clichéd. And they feel too psychiatric. There's a difficulty of articulating in a way that convinces yourself. And therefore, why would you say it to somebody else? So, the only recourse I had for thirty years was to stay silent. And try to change the subject or laugh it off."

At seventy-four years old, O'Brien credits the passage of time for him finally being able to write about his trauma in 2019's *Dad's Maybe Book*, a meditation on life that has been compared to Vonnegut's later-in-life book of ruminations, *A Man Without a*

Country. O'Brien hopes his teenage sons will one day read it and talk with him about his war experiences.

Knowing that not everyone can "use it" as effectively as he, O'Brien sympathizes for the veterans for whom persistent pain can be paralyzing. Although in principle he believes veterans should suffer as much as any person who copes with the traumas of life, he acknowledges that veterans with crippling PTSD should get help. "It's person-specific," he says. "You have to be careful about generalizations."

According to O'Brien, the PTSD diagnosis itself is part of the problem because it can sometimes remove the veteran from what Mellina would call the "mess" of everyday life. "PTSD is a fancy expression for what we all go through in the tragedies in our lives," O'Brien says. "Our mothers die. There's divorce and there are all the other things that are going to strike you. Of course, these things hurt. It's the *of courseness* of it. Of course you have trouble dealing with it."

CHAPTER TEN
WHAT'S WRONG WITH BILLY?

IN HER GROUNDBREAKING 1992 BOOK, *Trauma and Recovery*, Harvard professor Judith Herman, a psychiatrist and pioneering researcher, writes of an "endless present" that prisoners, such as author and chemist Primo Levi, who survived the Auschwitz concentration camp, experience. In Levi's words: "Our wisdom lay in 'not trying to understand,' not imagining the future, not tormenting ourselves as to how and when it would all be over; not asking questions of ourselves or others. . . . For living men, the units of time always have a value. . . . For us, history had stopped."

And, according to Herman, this "rupture in continuity between present and past frequently persists even after the prisoner is released." And if he or she remains in denial about the period of captivity and the associated trauma, "this disconnected fragment of the past remains fully alive . . .

"[E]ven years after liberation, the former prisoner continues to practice doublethink and to exist simultaneously in two realities, two points in time," she writes.

It sure sounds like what Mellina is talking about. It also sounds like Billy Pilgrim, who "was simultaneously on foot in Germany in 1944 and riding his Cadillac in 1967" in

Slaughterhouse-Five. It's Tralfamadorian thinking—a literary construction that Vonnegut may have created to tell his story and to bring Pilgrim to life but that also fits perfectly into our understanding of a PTSD flashback.

So, does Pilgrim have PTSD?

The flashback, or more generally "reliving the event," is one of the four major symptoms listed in the VA's National Center for PTSD brochure on the condition. The others are "avoiding things that remind you of the event," "having more negative thoughts and feelings than before," and "feeling on edge."

The VA brochure includes a "PTSD screen" questionnaire, which determines if the person taking it may have the prime symptoms. It advises that if a person were to answer "yes" to three or more of the five questions, he or she should talk to a mental health care provider. The brochure also states that however many answers are in the affirmative, it doesn't automatically mean the veteran does or doesn't have PTSD. "Only a mental health care provider can tell you for sure," it reads.

I ask Mellina to take the questionnaire and he answers "yes" to all five questions.

We agree that it would be interesting to subject Pilgrim to the questionnaire as well. "I feel like Vonnegut wanted to give personification to PTSD. And Billy Pilgrim was his way," Mellina says. "I think Vonnegut's PTSD is named Billy Pilgrim."

So I decided to give Billy Pilgrim the questionnaire.

SOMETIMES THINGS HAPPEN to people that are unusually or especially frightening, horrible, or traumatic. Have you ever experienced this kind of event?

According to Pilgrim, the first time he becomes unstuck in time is in 1944, when he is separated from his platoon and becomes a "dazed wanderer" during the Battle of the Bulge. When he is shot at, he stands politely because he believes the rules of war dictate that he should give the German soldier a fair crack at hitting him. He is beaten by his fellow American, Roland Weary. And then he is captured, and he suffers physically and emotionally during his time as a prisoner of war. He is exposed to immense pain and death among his fellow American prisoners and while he takes part in the burial and disposal of the thousands of German citizens who are killed at Dresden.

Answer: Yes. (I am not including how, later in his life, he is also the only survivor of a plane crash because he was showing signs of trauma well before that accident.)

Had nightmares about the event(s) or thought about the event(s) when you didn't want to?
A strong argument has been made by critics that many of Pilgrim's time-traveling episodes are actually him entering a dream state or having nightmares. When he experiences the initial time travel in 1944, he "could scarcely distinguish between sleep and wakefulness." This first so-called trip is to the sink-or-swim lesson by his father, being thrown into the pool, which he says feels like "an execution."

The next sequence in which he travels occurs when he is an optometrist and he falls asleep while seeing a patient, who asks him if he saw something "terrible." It's a lugubrious double entendre joke—the patient is asking if the reason Pilgrim went quiet was that he may have seen something terrible in her eyes—but we know that the terrible things that Pilgrim has been seeing are in his past.

Then he closes his eyes and travels in time again. This liminal space between sleep and being awake occurs numerous times. When Pilgrim is talking with his wife, Valencia, at night during their honeymoon, he gets out of bed and goes to the bathroom and trips back and forth from his wartime experience when he was in bed on morphine. When Valencia asks him to talk about his war experience, Pilgrim says, "It would sound like a dream."

What Pilgrim calls "being unstuck" can be interpreted as his dreams, his nightmares, and the simple act of remembering, which is, of course, a way of going mentally into the past. The closest that Pilgrim comes to being self-aware that he is fending off traumatic memories happens on his eighteenth wedding anniversary when the barbershop quartet of optometrists performs.

As they sing, Pilgrim becomes upset and has what the book's narrator calls "powerful psychosomatic responses." People think he's having a heart attack and Valencia says it looks as if he'd seen a ghost. He has no idea why the quartet's song affects him "so grotesquely," he thinks. "He had supposed for years that he had no secrets from himself. Here was proof that he had a great big secret somewhere inside," the narrator says.

When the quartet sings again, Pilgrim racks his brain for why it upsets him. He realizes that they remind him of the four German guards collectively reacting to the devastating bombing of their city above the slaughterhouse bunker. Their faces contorted in expressions that reminded Pilgrim of a barbershop quartet. Uncharacteristically, he does not travel in time here but instead "remembered it shimmeringly."

The incident is consistent with external psychological stimuli, also known as triggers, which cause PTSD sufferers to have
flashbacks. Triggers repeat throughout the book, connecting Pilgrim to his past, such as the color combinations ivory-white and
orange-black, or there are smells, such as the evocative mustard
gas and roses.

On so many levels, Pilgrim appears to be either having
nightmares or somehow revisiting his traumatic memories
through his subconscious.

Answer: Yes. That seems to be accurate.

*Tried hard not to think about the event(s) or went out of your way
to avoid situations that reminded you of the event(s)?*
Either Pilgrim is brought to Tralfamadore or he isn't. If it didn't
actually happen to the character, then it's fair to consider it an
elaborate attempt to avoid his past, whether it's intentional or
not. In that penultimate chapter of the book, Pilgrim's Dorothy-
in-Kansas experience in the porno shop strongly suggests that
Tralfamadore is a manifestation of his mind, and so the close
reader can deduce that Tralfamadore is Pilgrim's pleasant fabu-
lation to defend himself from the horrors that he has endured or
witnessed. The Tralfamadorians' providing Pilgrim with a curvy
porn star who happily has sex with him and eventually has a baby
with him is both wish fulfillment and avoidance.

Answer: Yes.

Been constantly on guard, watchful, or easily startled?
This isn't Pilgrim's affect. He is more dazed and inert. When he
enters the POW camp and is greeted by the British soldiers, his

coat catches fire and he hardly reacts, prompting one of them to say of him, "This isn't a man. It's a broken kite."

He is so fragile that he fears that he would "shatter like glass." He does, however, appear to be on guard in 1967, when he is in his office and a fire station siren goes off announcing it's noon. It scares "the hell out of him. He was expecting World War Three at any time."

Outside of that moment of jumpiness, the one time that Pilgrim isn't collapsing in on himself is when the British soldiers put on a comical rendition of "Cinderella" and he breaks into uncontrollable laughter to the point that he is tied down and given morphine to stop his constant shrieking.

But this does not generally describe Pilgrim.

Answer: No.

Felt numb or detached from people, activities, or your surroundings?
This is Pilgrim, who numbly stumbles his way through the war. When he doesn't want to be left alone to die, he sees the world not even like a child but more like an infant; he smiles at his fellow suffering American soldiers because he is hallucinating a radiant light around their heads.

"It was beautiful," he thinks. Pilgrim is "enchanted" by the glimpse of the Nazi guards' boxcar. He is utterly passive, accepting whatever happens to him. He is detached.

After the war, Pilgrim remains disassociated from everyone around him, as well as his own body and thoughts. He's not sure why he married his wife; "He knew he was going crazy when he heard himself proposing marriage to her," Vonnegut writes. When she tells him on their wedding night that she hadn't thought anyone would marry her, he can only muster, "Um." He doesn't seem to have any friends. Later in life, he is totally disconnected from his children.

When he's elected president of the Lions Club, he thinks his acceptance speech will make him sound like a "ludicrous waif" with a "reedy voice," but he's surprised by his own "deep, resonant" tone, which he attributes to a public speaking course he had previously taken.

As a middle-aged optometrist, he finds himself worried "about his mind in general. He tried to remember how old he was, couldn't. He tried to remember what year it was. He couldn't remember that, either." When he's older, his daughter berates him for not caring for himself, not noticing that his house had become cold because the furnace had broken.

Pilgrim's numbness and detachment are his defining traits. They are extensions of how he sees the world. On the wall in his optometry office, he has a saying that he says keeps him going, "even though he was unenthusiastic about living." It's the Serenity Prayer: "God grant me the serenity to accept the things I cannot change, courage to change the things I can, and wisdom to always tell the difference." At the end of the book, the same saying reappears on a pendant hanging from Montana Wildhack's neck.

The prayer so happens to have been appropriated by Alcoholics Anonymous. Is this a sly reference on Vonnegut's part? Either way, in his darkly ironic rendering, the inspirational words do nothing for Pilgrim, thanks to his adopted Tralfamadorian point of view on free will: "Among the things Billy Pilgrim could not change were the past, the present and the future," Vonnegut writes.

Most of all, Pilgrim's aghast yet accepting disposition is distilled in "So it goes."

Answer: Yes.

Felt guilty or unable to stop blaming yourself or others for the event(s) or any problems the event(s) may have caused?

Poor Pilgrim is hardly capable of such assertive emotions or thoughts as guilt and blame. The one time he seems demonstrably moved by the consequences of his own actions is when two German obstetricians tell him to get off the horse-drawn cart he's sitting on at the end of the war. They berate him for the condition of the horses pulling the wagon, pointing out what he hadn't noticed—that they are bleeding from the mouths, have broken hooves, and are dying of thirst. When Pilgrim sees their condition, he bursts into tears for the first time during the war.

We are told that he later constantly weeps, but we're not sure why.

Answer: This would probably be a no.

SO THAT'S THREE OUT OF FIVE affirmative answers that strongly suggest Pilgrim ought to see a mental health care provider, who should be able to see Pilgrim's war trauma on almost every page of *Slaughterhouse-Five.*

What may be less clear is how to diagnose his mental condition. Many critics concluded that Pilgrim is schizophrenic, a gray-area mental illness diagnosis that is still to this day being developed by the medical establishment. Schizophrenia has yet to be fully explained and could be caused by a combination of genetics and environmental triggers, including stress or trauma. The primary symptoms are social withdrawal, unresponsiveness, hallucinations, and delusions. English professor and author Lawrence Broer makes the case that Pilgrim is schizophrenic in his 1989 book, *Sanity Plea: Schizophrenia in the Novels of Kurt Vonnegut*.

Vonnegut's family history with mental illness makes mental health connections to his characters inevitable. It's an interpretation that Vonnegut teases at in his extended title to the book, which includes: "This is a novel somewhat in the telegraphic schizophrenic manner of tales of the planet Tralfamadore, where the flying saucers come from. Peace."

In 1973's *Breakfast of Champions*, the book that Vonnegut wrote after *Slaughterhouse-Five*, and which was partly derived from material he originally intended for Billy Pilgrim's story, the author inserts himself and says, "I mouthed this word: schizophrenia. The sound and appearance of the word had fascinated me for many years. It sounded and looked to me like a human being sneezing in a blizzard of soapflakes. I did not and do not know for certain that I have that disease."

And no wonder it was on his mind: Vonnegut's son, Mark, suffered a mental collapse in 1971, which was then considered to be a schizophrenic episode.

Three years after the war, Pilgrim suffers a "mild nervous collapse" and he goes to a veterans hospital for six months and is given shock therapy treatments. Very pointedly, his doctors don't think that the war has "anything" to do with his mental problems. They "were sure" his mental illness should be attributed to his childhood, in particular his sink-or-swim lesson and the trip to the Grand Canyon when he peed in his pants.

I read Vonnegut's jokey inclusion of this medical expert opinion as ironic, and therefore as a clear testament to his

Tom Lea's illustration appeared in *Life* magazine in June 1945.
That 2,000 Yard Stare. Oil on canvas, 36½ × 28½.
Life Collection of Art WWII, U.S. Army Center of Military History,
Fort Belvoir, Virginia. Image courtesy of the Tom Lea Institute.

intention that Pilgrim's derangement is *absolutely* rooted in his war experience. He says it by not saying it. According to Case Western Reserve University literature professor Susanne Vees-Gulani, who wrote the essay "Diagnosing Billy Pilgrim: A

Psychiatric Approach to Kurt Vonnegut's *Slaughterhouse-Five*," it was standard medical opinion in the 1940s to not attribute mental illness to external stimuli but instead to focus on how childhood events affected a person in later life.

Beyond the page, there is the fact that Vonnegut used Joe Crone, a soldier traumatized by war, as the model for Pilgrim. "He died of what is called the 'thousand-mile stare,'" Vonnegut told interviewer Lee Roloff in 1996. "People did this same thing in prison war camps, dying of the thousand-mile stare. When one chooses the thousand-mile stare, this is what happens: the person sits down on the floor with his back to the wall, will not talk, will not eat, and just stares into the space in front of him."

The exact origination of the term "thousand-mile stare" is difficult to determine, but it was made popular in June 1945, the month that Vonnegut returned to Indiana, when *Life* magazine published a graphic article featuring the visceral artwork of painter Tom Lea, who depicted US soldiers during the bloody invasion of the island of Peleliu, which was occupied by thousands of entrenched Japanese troops.

It was one of the most costly battles for the United States, which, despite successfully winning the island, suffered more than 1,500 dead and nearly 7,000 wounded. Two entire US regiments were so depleted they were deemed "combat ineffective."

Lea's artwork in *Life* shows Americans dying, struggling, and fighting grimly, complemented by his captions in which he reported the emotional toll. One of the illustrations, captioned *Battle Fatigue*, showed a hollow-eyed soldier staring starkly ahead. Lea's caption reads, "He half-sleeps at night and gouges Japs out of holes all day. Two-thirds of his company has been killed or wounded but he is still standing. So he will return to attack this morning. How much can a human being endure?"

Lea, who later said he had noticed the soldier "staring stiffly at nothing. His mind had crumbled in battle," named the painting *That 2000 Yard Stare.*

It is likely that Vonnegut had seen or knew of the painting, but whether he did or not, he recognized the same trauma-induced stare in Crone that Lea had seen on the island of Peleliu. And they both used the same language to describe a condition that shaped Billy Pilgrim. Today, we'd call the 2,000-yard—or thousand-mile—stare an indicator of post-traumatic stress disorder.

If we want to give a name to Pilgrim's mental illness, I believe the evidence shows that his condition is rooted in his war experience and therefore it's best to call it war trauma. In his day, it would have been referred to as combat neurosis and combat fatigue, but if he were alive today, as we see with the questionnaire, doctors would probably call it PTSD.

CHAPTER ELEVEN
DIAGNOSING MR. VONNEGUT

"HE HAD PTSD!"

That was the epiphany Venice Beach artist Lance Miccio said out loud while working in his studio on his painting *Poor Old Edgar Derby* in 2016, part of a series of fifty pieces honoring *Slaughterhouse-Five*'s fiftieth anniversary. He wrote down the letters *P, T, S, D,* and underlined them. "I had it all in front of me, all of these bodies and smoking buildings. And Edgar Derby is about to be shot for picking up a teapot. I realized the horror of it," Miccio says. "For Vonnegut to write this book, he'd been struggling with it. It's so graphic. He was detaching himself in a way so that he could tell it. It came out of his PTSD."

Sixty-year-old Miccio had read the book several times before. He was a big fan, enough to have come up with the idea of doing the fifty paintings to honor the anniversary, but he hadn't made the PTSD connection before, which isn't entirely surprising, because he hadn't even recognized that he had the same condition himself.

Not that his wife and adult daughter hadn't suggested it to him many times before. Or that his life hadn't been impacted; Miccio had believed that his daughter didn't like to visit him because he thought that she didn't want to deal with his manic behavior and emotional outbursts. And his sleep had been haunted by night sweats and nightmares for decades.

Miccio hasn't lost his thick, flat, fast-talking Sheepshead Bay, Brooklyn, accent despite living under the Southern California sun for the past fifteen years. Otherwise, he's blended in well; he's a painter, teacher, and filmmaker with his hands in many aesthetic mediums. He has produced and directed documentaries and feature films, and his self-described *Krazy Kat*–meets–Van Gogh paintings have drawn a Hollywood clientele that includes actor John Lithgow, with whom he does an annual *Moby-Dick* reading with other Venice Beach artists.

He also runs a madcap cannabis Wiffle ball league. (Teams include the Brooklyn Bong Squad, the Chicago Kush, the Detroit Dabs, and the Philly Blunts.) And he is an inspired chemist with cannabis extracts. He spreads cannabis butter on toast for his morning tonic and then has more at night to help him sleep.

Growing up in Brooklyn, Miccio first discovered *Slaughterhouse-Five* in 1976 in Mr. Shweky's eleventh-grade English class. He loved it then, but it grew to be more important to him later. Miccio comes from a family of firefighters and cops—one of his grandfathers was gunned down in the New York City streets by the mob—and he put on a uniform for the navy, which he joined in 1979 as a submariner. Life in an underwater tin can meant Cold War exercises that weren't called exercises; he was trained to constantly face the potentiality of nuclear war.

Miccio got kicked off his vessel for smoking pot and was assigned in 1982 to a "gator freighter," the USS *Guam*, an amphibious ship, where, ironically, the sailors suspected Miccio of being NIS (Naval Investigative Services, the internal law enforcement agency that preceded the NCIS), because there was a bootleg operation on the boat and the sailor whom Miccio replaced had died from drinking illegal hooch. Miccio joined the *Guam* just as it was going on a peacekeeping mission to Lebanon that became a humanitarian one after all hell broke loose. Israel and various militias were engaged in a civil war that killed and injured thousands, devastating the region.

The *Guam* helped transport Palestinian militants out of the country as part of an agreement and went to Spain before heading back to Lebanon, where Miccio spent almost a week loading and unloading supplies for the marines in his role as a storekeeper.

On shore one night, Miccio was driving a jeep with a Marine sergeant after a supply run, when they got lost. Driving through the rubble and bombed-out neighborhoods of Beirut was harrowing. Miccio was so scared that at times he couldn't control his body. When he wasn't driving, he slipped his hands underneath his thighs while his legs jumped spastically. He was sure there were militants around every corner. He stopped the jeep several times and felt like he could smell death. Rats crawled everywhere. For more than forty-five minutes, Miccio was terrified. Finally, they found their way back, unscathed but shaken.

Not long after leaving the navy, Miccio began to have a recurring sweat-inducing nightmare. In the dream, he is usually lost or wandering in a shabby part of town; it could be Beirut, Detroit, or somewhere in Winnipeg. He is petrified and often he finds himself seated on his hands, just as he was back in the jeep, with his legs bouncing frantically. Often he is being chased. Sometimes he has committed some sort of atrocity and he is going to be court-martialed. For almost forty years, two or three times a week, he would wake up drenched in sweat.

Lance Miccio in his Venice Beach studio. *Pow Tweet*, one of the paintings from
his *Slaughterhouse-Five* series, is behind him.
Courtesy of Lance Miccio.

Despite the recurring night terrors, the cannabis self-
medication regimen, and a tendency to get irrationally livid over
the smallest things, like how his eggs might be cooked one morning, Miccio never considered that he might be suffering from
trauma stemming from his military service.

"I never really thought about it. Okay, I get dreams, but I learned to live with it," Miccio says. "You almost feel guilty saying anything bothers you if you weren't really in it. I never saw actual combat. It's embarrassing."

Miccio and I spoke for the first time in November 2019 when we met in Indianapolis for the opening of the new home for the Kurt Vonnegut Museum and Library, where Miccio's fifty *Slaughterhouse-Five* paintings premiered. His cousin Joey was with him and we spoke while watching a Jets game at a bar called Ralston's Drafthouse. Miccio told me about the recurring nightmares and he excitedly recalled several memories that may not have been combat but were disturbing nonetheless.

When the USS *Guam* docked off of the US naval station in Rota, Spain, Miccio went ashore with hundreds of other sailors and marines who were on R & R. There was massive drinking and lots of brawling between the marines and the navy sailors. Miccio says he was ambushed outside a bar by a group of marines who, he suspects, were paid off by a fellow sailor from his ship who thought Miccio was investigating the illegal liquor trade on board. Miccio got beat up pretty bad but, according to him, the four marines ended up worse: After they had gotten their licks in and had left him on the ground, he jumped all four of them with a piece of concrete in his hand and sent all of them to the infirmary. He'd been in plenty of scraps before, but this was a different degree of violence than he'd ever been a part of.

There were other ugly incidents: Two sailors he knew were killed in a bomb blast. Miccio didn't experience the explosion, but he vividly recalls going to the infirmary and looking at the swollen head of one of his buddies, oozing fluids before he died. He also remembers dead human and animal bodies floating in the harbor. And, in general, the mission weighed heavily on his conscience: After the Palestinian militants were convinced to be evacuated to Tunisia, their families were slaughtered in the ensuing fighting. It was Miccio's job to help supply the equipment for the marines to remove the dead families that had been left behind.

At the Indianapolis airport, the day after Miccio and I spoke, we bumped into each other and he told me that he woke up again in a sweat, but this time the night terror was much worse than what he was used to.

"How can I be whining about this when other guys are losing their legs? I never really thought that it could apply to me," he said. "Maybe I'll go to a therapist. It was a weird breakthrough for me. But I did probably have the worst night of my life last night."

It was hard to get his head around. "I did nothing heroic. I was just there," he said of Lebanon. "But I recognized what was going on. It was wholesale slaughter and death. And it was a moon landscape. That's why *Slaughterhouse* became more important to me over the years. Maybe I am doing the same thing, working through something."

Miccio's earlier epiphany about Vonnegut was coming more into focus. "What's he going to say, 'I got PTSD because I got frostbite on my feet'? It was hard for him," Miccio said as we waited for our planes. "It's weakness. If you are an alpha male—and the guys who go to war are going to be alpha—then you are not keen to admit weakness. But Kurt had PTSD."

MUCH OF the literary establishment has come to the same conclusion about the author. "Critics generally recognize that the war, particularly the destruction of Dresden, had a traumatizing effect on Vonnegut," writes Case Western Reserve University's Vees-Gulani in "Diagnosing Billy Pilgrim." "Vonnegut's writing of *Slaughterhouse-Five* can be seen as a therapeutic process that allows him to uncover and deal with his trauma."

There are some dissenters, however, notably members of Vonnegut's generation. Vonnegut's friend Dan Wakefield, also an author from Indianapolis, is dubious, although he allows that it's a valid interpretation. Jerome Klinkowitz is more resolute: "Kurt didn't have it. I don't really think even Billy Pilgrim has it," he says. "But Joe Crone obviously had PTSD."

According to Klinkowitz, the emphasis on what makes *Slaughterhouse-Five* tick shouldn't be armchair psychological diagnoses of Vonnegut's PTSD but literary approaches to the "imaginary construct" that he created to tell the story, which is, most fundamentally, "a way to spatialize time." The notion of being unstuck in time and of the Tralfamadorian view of the universe (time isn't sequential; free will doesn't exist) is what carries the novel, a literary conceit that allows Vonnegut to tell his postmodern tale.

And yet, Klinkowitz acknowledges that Vonnegut's accomplishment dovetails with a soldier coping with a traumatic disorder: "You are sitting here in 2019 and you're feeling okay but something you experienced in 2003 in Afghanistan is frying you and that's because time is sequential. We are sentenced to the sequence of time. It is hard to handle trauma in terms of time, but you can handle it in terms of space if you put it all together on the same plane like an artistic collage."

But the PTSD analysis of *Slaughterhouse-Five* and Vonnegut is too reductive and clinical for Klinkowitz, who is disappointed that this point of view has overtaken the way people discuss the book and author today.

Klinkowitz is in the minority. Two of the most compelling voices that support the Vonnegut-had-PTSD position are two of Vonnegut's children, Mark and Nanette, who are adamant on the subject.

"I think a majority of great art is people struggling mightily against something like mental illness," Mark Vonnegut tells me over the phone. "PTSD is a mental illness. It's an acquired mental illness.

"I don't think the death of his mother was traumatic," Mark adds. "I think the death of his sister was just something that happened. I don't think it was traumatic. I think being beaten by the Germans and experiencing Dresden, that's traumatic."

After what was dubbed Mark's schizophrenic break in 1971, he's had several episodes, and he has settled on the term *bipolar* for his condition. In addition to becoming a successful pediatrician, Mark has written two critically acclaimed books about his mental health issues, *The Eden Express* and *Just Like Someone Without Mental Illness Only More So*. He has more than just a son's understanding of his father's mental state.

"There's no blood test for PTSD," he says. "He definitely had depression. But what's the cause and what's the result? The man definitely drank too much. PTSD is as good a description as you're going to find."

Whether or not Vonnegut had PTSD wouldn't be as relevant a question if he hadn't put himself so squarely in the novel. The author/narrator/Vonnegut character presents himself as having had the harrowing experiences of being captured by Nazis, being put in a POW camp, and enduring the bombing of Dresden. And he writes of himself drinking late at night, calling people in the wee hours, and experiencing severe memory lapses. He sounds melancholy but he's completed this book, so, even if he dismisses it as a failure, there is the suggestion that he is coping pretty well—even if it took him twenty-three years. A late breakthrough is better than none at all.

In the pages of *Slaughterhouse-Five*, Vonnegut's presentation of himself could be interpreted in various ways, but I think it's reasonable for readers, if they want to, to believe that he had been traumatized. Beyond the book, we have more information; what we know of Vonnegut includes a family history of mental illness, the tragedy of his mother's death, and further confirmation that he drank enough to be considered an alcoholic.

In 1973, he reflected on how "about every 20 days, I blew my cork," he said. "I thought for a long time that I had perfectly good reasons for these periodic blowups; I thought people around me had it coming to them. But only recently have I realized that this has been happening regularly since I've been six years old."

Numerous times, Vonnegut spoke of periods of being "profoundly depressed," and that he saw psychiatrists and took medication for depression. And in 1984, his second wife, Jill Krementz, discovered him unconscious after he had ingested a near-lethal dose of alcohol, sleeping pills, and antidepressants. He had scribbled a note saying he'd leave it to Jill and Jane to fight over his will. Charles Shields, in his *And So It Goes*, portrays the suicide attempt as a half-hearted act of revenge during a tense period with Krementz.

What makes a person attempt suicide? What makes a person tick? These are the sorts of questions that Vonnegut confronted in his writing. He wrote of the chemicals in his characters' brains, and often likened humans' biochemical impulses to robot-like wiring that makes us who we are. It would be nonsense to suggest that Vonnegut wasn't plumbing his own psyche to unravel how he'd write about the human mind, especially in a semiautobiographical novel.

Sure, it's said that "art is not biography." But there is also truth in the notion that "every painter paints him- or herself."

In the drafts of *Slaughterhouse-Five* at the Lilly Library, there is a version of the first-person first chapter in which Vonnegut wrote, "I suppose that I was slightly crazy when I got home from that war," and he tells a story of going to a cocktail party in Indianapolis where the conversation drifted to the news that a "lady librarian" had been killed in her apartment the night before. In this draft, this struck Vonnegut as hilarious and he couldn't stop laughing. "Nobody at the party had realized that the murder had a comical side. One woman there still couldn't see anything funny about it. She told me that I made her sick."

Using a fictionalized version of himself that Vonnegut didn't publish to support my assessment of him may seem like quite a stretch if the representation weren't so consistent with everything else we know about Vonnegut and have read by him. He repeatedly poked and prodded at the notion of war-induced trauma.

And yet, he also always denied that the trauma could apply to him. He had war experiences that the US Army, in the PTSD questionnaire, would clearly call "unusually or especially frightening, horrible, or traumatic." And although he wasn't known to have nightmares—his daughter Nanette tells me that her father "said he slept like a baby and noted Winston Churchill did too"—his heavy drinking and phone calls late at night could suggest that he was trying "hard not to think about the event."

Applying the questionnaire to Vonnegut isn't conclusive. The author wasn't known to be jumpy, but he certainly "detached" himself from people. He was a writer, after all! And one could go either way in asserting that Vonnegut felt "guilt" when considering his "astonishment" and near obsession with how America bombed Dresden and then let it be largely forgotten. His interest in the subject and determination to write the book could suggest he couldn't let go of the events, which may be a sign of PTSD, but to Tim O'Brien not letting go shouldn't be defined as unhealthy. "You should remember," O'Brien says to me. "I think that's true in Vonnegut's case because he wrote a beautiful novel about it. He couldn't have written it if he had put it all behind him."

Central to the clinical diagnosis of PTSD is whether or not there is "impairment" in "important areas of functioning." Vonnegut functioned better than most of us. He was a highly productive writer, a consistently celebrated public speaker, and a socially involved person. So I think that there is only one legitimate answer to applying the army's PTSD questionnaire to Vonnegut.

Answer: Well, maybe. But maybe not.

Vonnegut adamantly refuted the suggestion that his wartime experiences had an impact on him personally. "If I told him he had PTSD, he'd tell me to go soak my head," Mark Vonnegut says.

Vonnegut rarely spoke or wrote directly about what he actually felt during the war. The closest we come to hearing from him may be in the letter written by his uncle Alex in 1945, when the young Vonnegut tearfully exclaimed, "The sons of bitches! The sons of bitches!" after telling his family the story of Michael Palaia.

In one unusually candid interview in 1996, Vonnegut admitted, "I saw a hell of a lot of death, and I saw a hell of a lot of it during the Battle of the Bulge when my division was wiped out. But then in Dresden I saw a mountain of dead people. And that makes you thoughtful."

Thoughtful. Talk about an understatement. But just as this suggests he is admitting something intimately, painfully personal, Vonnegut adds, "It . . . made . . . you think about . . . death. I have said, too, that I would not have missed it for the world. It was a hell of an adventure. You know, as long as you [are] going to see something, see something really thought provoking."

Vonnegut was never one to accept the boxes that others tried to put him in. And I believe he didn't want to be pinned down as another writer traumatized by war. "I suppose you'd think so, because that's the cliché," he told *Playboy* in 1973. "The importance of Dresden in my life has been considerably exaggerated because my book about it became a bestseller. If the book hadn't been a bestseller, it would seem like a very minor experience in my life. And I don't think peoples' lives are changed by short term events like that. Dresden was astonishing, but experiences can be astonishing without changing you."

Calling what he witnessed during the war a "minor experience" seems like Vonnegut doth protest too much. And there is plenty of clinical evidence that a "short term" experience, if it is harrowing enough, can in fact forever change a person. But Vonnegut's position remained consistent. He wrote in 1981's *Palm Sunday*: "Being present at the destruction of Dresden has affected my character far less than the death of my mother, the adopting of my sister's children, the sudden realization that those children and my own were no longer dependent on me, the breakup of my marriage, and so on."

I tracked down an English teacher named Karen English because I heard from another source that she loved to teach *Slaughterhouse-Five* and tried to include it in her courses when she could. She recently retired as a humanities professor at San Jose State University, where she worked for close to thirty years. She warns me about giving too much credence to Vonnegut's denials. "We are not the best judges of ourselves. I know that other people's views of me are different from my own view of myself," she says. "And authors are not always the best critics and analysts of their own writing."

English sees the possibility for healing for both Pilgrim, the character, as well Vonnegut, the author. She and her students looked at that moment toward the end of the book when the protagonist has that explicitly traumatic reaction at his wedding anniversary with the barbershop quartet. Throughout the book he passively floats through time jumps, but Vonnegut appears to highlight the fact that, here, Pilgrim remembers something "shimmeringly."

"I don't think Vonnegut could have written that narrative moment without understanding the process of healing from trauma," English says. "If healing trauma is about shaping it through narrative, then that is what happens when Vonnegut is finally able to write this book and put himself in the book as both a fictional character and a real one. And he treats Billy as his avatar. Then, yeah, writing the book for Vonnegut the historical person is doing what remembering Dresden does for the fictional character Billy in this crazy postmodern book."

English believes that Vonnegut, the historical person, did experience trauma. And she suggests he may have found healing through writing the book. "That's the theory today, right? That narrative can be part of the process of healing."

TWO WEEKS after talking with Lance Miccio in Indianapolis, he sent me a text. "Don't know why exactly but it could be as simple as identifying the source. But since our last conversation at airport," he wrote, "I have not had my being chased dream which I had on a semi daily basis. Which is awesome."

Nine months later, still nothing. He attributed the change to our conversation, when for the first time he connected his violent brawl with getting lost in Beirut. Plus, there was his high-stress duty on the submarine. He also cited the "cathartic" meeting of Vonnegut lovers in Indianapolis, which included a daughter relaying her experiences with her veteran father-in-law with PTSD in a fictional story. "You don't understand," the father had said to her of how he couldn't sleep at night. "I don't because you never told me," responded the daughter.

Miccio, whose own daughter repeatedly told him he had PTSD, could relate. "I guess we don't see ourselves for what we really are," he said.

"I thought I wasn't enough in the shit to get PTSD but all the things together built up in my psyche," he said of his experiences while in the service. "I had never thought it connected. I pieced it all together."

I asked Miccio to take the same questionnaire that I gave to Mellina, Pilgrim, and Vonnegut. Miccio confirmed four, possibly five, of the five symptoms. The one that he didn't think he had was detachment, because he's such a hyper-engaged, social person.

He surprised me when he said he believed he had survivor's guilt. We hadn't discussed at all his feeling about the 241

US soldiers, mostly marines, who were tragically killed in the bombing of their barracks in 1983, which happened right after the *Guam* had left the region. He told me that during his night terrors he would wake up and sometimes say Hail Mary prayers for his friends who died in that attack, the worst mass killing of US soldiers since World War II. Their deaths also reinforced Miccio's guilt for feeling any glimmer of trauma from anything he had experienced in the navy.

Miccio emailed me work-in-progress photos of his *Dresden Was Like the Moon* painting from his *Slaughterhouse-Five* series, adding, "Brought to you by Kurt Vonnegut, PTSD, mushrooms, edible cannabis, many bong hits of ganja and about an ounce of red Lava Cake hash from Navajo nation and about 12 pounds of coffee and English tea."

Miccio is aware that he self-medicates with drugs and his painting. "I never thought [about] why I paint so much, but it is this time when I am not thinking," he says. This would, in fact, loop us back to the issue of detachment. When he paints for hours, Miccio is removed from the world. He enters what he calls "a trance." How this PTSD symptom may differ from the others is that Miccio has used it as part of his creative process. It's actually a positive factor in his life—not unlike, perhaps, a certain writer we know who banged away at his Smith-Corona for hours on end, day after day, year after year.

After we met in Indianapolis, Miccio attended some PTSD group sessions at the VA in Los Angeles, but he didn't feel comfortable. "It was too much for me," he says. "These guys have real stuff going on. Lost an eye. IEDs. And I'm like, 'Uh. I got my feelings hurt.'"

The more Miccio tells me about his acknowledgment of his own PTSD and his progress, the more it reminds me of Vonnegut. Miccio agrees. "He declared himself a Roosevelt Democrat. He kept things to himself. You don't whine. You don't complain." Miccio adds that Vonnegut must have also felt ashamed for having surrendered, a further obstacle to the author admitting he had any trauma, even if laying down his weapons was the smart thing to do. "Surrendering without firing a shot is not how any soldier wants to go," Miccio says.

In the late 1980s, Miccio had told his cousin Joey, who came with him to Indiana, about his dustup with the marines. Miccio says his cousin didn't believe him and so he stopped talking about it. When I spoke with Joey, he told me about his experiences as a firefighter in New York City during the September 11 attacks. Joey lost friends that day. He told me he sometimes goes to therapy about it, something he'd never told Lance before.

Lance's brother is a firefighter who was also at the World Trade Center on September 11. His best friend, another firefighter, was standing right next to him when he was killed. Lance's brother never talks to him about it.

That's a lot of pain being kept under the surface.

After we talked, Lance asked his eighty-year-old father, a former firefighter, if he ever has night terrors. "Yes," he joked. "I dream that Plaxico Burress dropped Eli [Manning]'s wide-open TD pass against the Pats" in Super Bowl XLII."

Poof. Trauma disappears with a joke. Vonnegut also turned trauma into a joke by mocking it with a filthy flamingo of a protagonist and toilet plunger–like aliens. Robert Jay Lifton, the psychiatrist who helped develop the PTSD diagnosis, says that

Vonnegut's jeering and jousting is a way of mastering trauma. Lifton credited *Slaughterhouse-Five* with "the exalted possibilities of mockery" in his "Survivor as Creator" essay.

Some critics have written that Billy Pilgrim's catatonic state is reflective of a nihilism that Vonnegut himself felt about the world. David Morris, author of *The Evil Hours*, says that *Slaughterhouse-Five* was "ahead of its time," but he is still troubled by its "disturbing quietism and moral resignation."

Author and critic Anthony Burgess is the best known of those who have accused the book of "quietism," or resigned acceptance. Burgess, who claimed that he couldn't even finish the book, told an interviewer in 1974 that *Slaughterhouse-Five* "is a kind of evasion—in a sense, like J. M. Barrie's *Peter Pan*—in which we're being told to carry the horror of the Dresden bombing, and everything it implies, up to a level of fantasy, which means that neither the fantasy nor the realism works."

Lifton and others see it very differently. "So it goes," for example, is not false sentimentalism or a mere shrug of the shoulders. "Vonnegut uses the phrase all through the book with a combination of gaiety and terror," Lifton writes, "as a form of mocking witness to man's unfeeling murders, to his equally unfeeling survival of those murders, and to precisely the resignation that the phrase suggests.

"What I am suggesting is that to 'touch death' and then rejoin the living can be a source of insight and power," Lifton continues. "The vision of death gives life. The vision of total annihilation makes it possible to imagine living . . . beyond that curse."

I ask Lifton to reflect on how Vonnegut was able to write a book that so adeptly predicts the PTSD diagnosis and whether or not it could be used as evidence that Vonnegut himself had PTSD.

"I don't have any clear answer to how he could do it," Lifton says. "What I would say is that his experience in Dresden created a permanent imprint which dominated his life after that. It was so extreme that everything he subsequently experienced was in some sense filtered through that Dresden exposure.

"He found an unusual way of doing that," he adds, "with a mocking imagination that he seems to have possessed and used very effectively."

I remind Lifton that Vonnegut repeatedly denied the impact of Dresden on him. "I don't believe for a moment that anything influenced him more or had as powerful an impact on his imagination as his Dresden exposure," Lifton says, before echoing what others have told me: "You can't always go by what a writer says about his writing."

So would he say that Vonnegut had PTSD?

"I think it depends on how you look at PTSD and if you want to be precise or if you want to use it more loosely. So I could understand either position," he says. "Yes, he had tendencies. But I would say 'No' to the question. He had symptoms coming from trauma but I wouldn't all too conveniently put him in the PTSD category."

I agree. The question of whether or not Vonnegut had PTSD reminds me of something Jerome Klinkowitz said about literary analysis: "Traditional literature teaches us that with a work of art, you cracked a nut and when you get to the meat, that's the truth. From the 1960s on, you don't crack a nut. What you do is you peel layers of an onion until there's nothing left."

That doesn't mean there is no truth. It's just that the truth is in those peels, and in the peeling itself. That's where we find Vonnegut.

CHAPTER TWELVE
KURT, AFTER THE CRUSADE

"THE CONFLICT BETWEEN the will to deny horrible events and the will to proclaim them aloud is the central dialectic of psychological trauma," writes professor Judith Herman in *Trauma and Recovery.* "The ordinary response to atrocities is to banish them from consciousness. Certain violations of the social compact are too terrible to utter aloud: this is the meaning of the word *unspeakable.*"

Slaughterhouse-Five's ability to resolve this conflict has been the subject of this book. There may be distinct and necessary differences between how psychiatrists and artists approach trauma, but there are also similarities, including this essential question of how one speaks the unspeakable. And Vonnegut may not have been thinking in Herman's terms, but he found his way; he doesn't deny it, nor does he proclaim it from the parapets. He goes at it sideways with dark humor and by subverting conventional structures of time, storytelling, and genre.

There is much to laud about Vonnegut's inventive, humane, and funny novel, but it is its ability to represent the deep cracks of war trauma that make it a true war story that you feel in your gut.

Tim O'Brien agrees that *Slaughterhouse-Five* adheres to his *Things They Carried* dictum by not lying about war: "If at the end of a war story you feel uplifted or if you feel that some small bit of rectitude has been salvaged from the larger waste, then you have been made the victim of a very old and terrible lie."

He admires Vonnegut's "fidelity to how awful war is" and to "how numbing all those dead people [in Dresden] are," O'Brien says. "He handled how improbable it all seemed in a familiar way to me. With magical realism; other planets and time warps and that sort of thing. Time warp replicated my experience of the war seeming both yesterday and a million years ago."

O'Brien says he was not directly influenced by Vonnegut's writing—he tried reading one of his earlier novels, he thinks it may have been *The Sirens of Titan*, and was turned off—but eventually he read *Slaughterhouse-Five* and was "happy and surprised" to see that the two authors apply "different angles on the same psychological experience," he says. "The dissociative experience where your own memories seem improbable, although intellectually you know they're real memories. And how memory and imagination interplay. And that happens to all of us but perhaps more acutely when you are remembering moments of great trauma."

In his *Slaughterhouse-Five* fiftieth anniversary talk, Salman Rushdie gets at this just right: "One of the great questions that faces all writers who have to deal with atrocity is, is it possible to do it? Are there things so powerful, so dreadful, that they are beyond the power of literature to describe? Every writer who faced the challenge of writing about the Second World War—and the Vietnam War, in fact—has had to think about that question. All of them decided they needed to come at the atrocity at an angle, so to speak, not to face it head on, because to do that would be unbearable."

Rushdie identifies Vonnegut's "angle" as where his grim sense of humor, penetrating intellect, profound compassion, and subversive creativity meet. "He had a horror of people who took things too seriously and was simultaneously obsessed with the consideration of the most serious things, things both philosophical (like free will) and lethal (like the firebombing of Dresden). This is the paradox out of which his dark ironies grow. Nobody who futzed around so often and in so many ways with the idea of free will, or who cared so profoundly about the dead, could be described as a fatalist, or a quietist, or resigned. His books argue about ideas of freedom and mourn the dead, from their first pages to their last."

The original Crusades were medieval wars fought by Christians to reclaim the Holy Land from Muslims. Vonnegut mocked them by turning the concept of a war for a higher cause on its head by calling his book "The Children's Crusade: A Duty-Dance with Death," a subtitle he appropriated from an actual crusade by the same name that, in his *Slaughterhouse-Five* retelling, was a corrupt ruse in which thirty thousand children were misled into thinking they were fighting for their God and either died on the way or were sold into slavery. Vonnegut's alternate title is a condemnation of his war that was fought by young men not much older than children and as an ironic reference to those earlier acts of bloodshed. He wanted to expose the barbarity of all wars. But Vonnegut's struggle to write *Slaughterhouse-Five* was his own twenty-three-year crusade—his long war with its own higher, if secular, calling—to shape his war experiences into a true story.

"I FELT after I finished *Slaughterhouse-Five* that I didn't have to write at all anymore if I didn't want to," he said in 1973. "It was the end of some sort of career. I don't know why, exactly. I suppose that flowers, when they're through blooming, have some sort of awareness of some purpose having been served. Flowers didn't ask to be flowers and I didn't ask to be me. At the end of *Slaughterhouse-Five*, I had the feeling that I had produced this blossom. So I had a shutting-off feeling, you know, that I had done what I was supposed to do and everything was OK. And that was the end of it. I could figure out my missions for myself after that."

Vonnegut eventually gave himself an "A-plus" for *Slaughterhouse-Five* when he mischievously graded his own work, "comparing myself with myself," up to 1981's *Palm Sunday*. (He gave *Breakfast of Champions* a C, *Slapstick* got a D, and *Cat's Cradle* also earned an A-plus.) But the ultimate arbiter of Vonnegut's success was to be all those readers—from the critics to the book-buying public—whom he had been trying to reach ever since he decided to become a writer. And he finally broke through. Just nine months after filing the final draft, and after it had been released in serial format in *Ramparts* magazine, *Slaughterhouse-Five* was published and became an immediate hit, selling out the ten thousand copies of the first edition and launching onto the *New York Times* bestseller list for months in 1969.

"Serious critics have shown some reluctance to acknowledge that Vonnegut is among the best writers of his generation," Robert Scholes wrote in the front-page review of the book in the *New York Times Book Review*. "He is, I suspect, both too funny and too intelligent for many, who confuse muddled earnestness with profundity. Vonnegut is not confused. He sees all too clearly."

Most critics agreed with Scholes. And the book was such a success with young people at the height of the youth rebellion that Vonnegut was vaulted to superstar status, making him the unlikely paternal spokesman for a younger generation. This was an era when authors and intellectuals, such as Gore Vidal, Norman Mailer, and James Baldwin, were central to the national conversation through their books and articles and as guests on talk shows such as *The Dick Cavett Show* and William F. Buckley Jr.'s *Firing Line*. In 1969, Vonnegut was featured everywhere, from *60 Minutes* to talking with Walter Cronkite on TV for the moon landing on July 20, when he enraged many viewers by demonstrating his freethinking by criticizing the money spent on space exploration instead of ameliorating poverty.

But Vonnegut was speaking the dissenters' truth that many Americans were hungry for. Money began pouring in. Film companies optioned his past books. He signed deals for television projects. Actor Peter Fonda came by to discuss optioning *Cat's Cradle*. Vonnegut bought himself a Mercedes-Benz. It was a dizzying time, professionally and personally. Vonnegut adored the 1972 movie adaptation of *Slaughterhouse-Five* by director George Roy Hill. The film wasn't a hit at the box office, but it got good reviews and extended Vonnegut's popularity with college kids.

And yet, despite the rewards of success, Vonnegut was unhappy at home in Massachusetts. His marriage had been dissolving for years; the two years he'd spent at Iowa had only extended the decline. He was tired of fighting with Jane. The last family Christmas together was in 1969 and it was a fraught one. Everyone got drunk, according to Mark Vonnegut, who told Charles Shields, "The magic that had filled the Barnstable house was dying."

Vonnegut had his eyes on New York City. He had a project there that he was excited about; his play, *Happy Birthday, Wanda*

June, was going to have a run off-Broadway in the Village. "I was writing myself a new family and a new early manhood," he later wrote of the play. *Wanda June* moved to Broadway for a short run. Most critics, and even Vonnegut, weren't impressed by the production. His new family of actors may have been short-lived, but a relationship with photographer Jill Krementz, whom he met during rehearsals and eventually married in 1979, would be lifelong.

By the beginning of 1971, Vonnegut had moved permanently to New York, where he stepped, if not directly into the slipstream, perhaps onto the outer banks of the cultural elite. He met George Plimpton and palled around with friends, such as writers Joseph Heller and Sidney Offit and *60 Minutes'* Morley Safer. He was tickled by how his daughter Edith, an artsy girl-about-town, was also being swept up by the city. Edith would join her father at literary hotspot restaurant Elaine's. She married up-and-coming newsman Geraldo Rivera before the year was through. (They divorced four years later.)

Vonnegut was invited to teach writing at Harvard, which he happily groused about. It was, after all, the ultimate form of acceptance. Mark said that his father enjoyed the experience because "it gave him a chance to know people who were at home in the world."

In total, more than a million of his books had been sold when the *New York Times Magazine* sent a writer to profile him at Cambridge in the fall of 1970, where he appeared to be red-eyed, gregarious, sometimes snippy, yet laughing often—a "contradiction of moods," according to writer Richard Todd.

"Money is dumped on me, great quantities of money. I don't want it. I do, kind of," Vonnegut says in the article. "I am in the dangerous position now where I can sell anything I write. . . . For so long money motivated me and now there is nothing to move me off center. I don't know what to do."

Vonnegut fretted that he would lose the ability to write. "My intuition will pooh out—my creative craziness; there will be fewer pretty accidents in my writing. I'll become more of an explainer and less of a shower," he said.

He was particularly worried about the novel he was working on, *Breakfast of Champions*, but hoping that the rapid changes in his life would create an opportunity to change himself. "I think my wind is still good enough for me to go chasing after happiness, something I've never really tried," he said. "I get more respect for Truman Capote as the years go by, probably because he's becoming genuinely wiser all the time. I saw him on television the other night, and he said most good artists were stupid about almost everything but their arts. [Actor] Kevin McCarthy said nearly the same thing to me one time when I congratulated him for moving well in a play. He said, 'Most actors are very clumsy offstage.' I want to stop being stupid in real life. I want to stop being clumsy offstage."

But whatever creative puzzle he solved by telling the story of Billy Pilgrim couldn't make him whole. "He was just a guy who couldn't blend in and had to keep making up different stories about it," Mark says of his father, who went on to live a life that may not have been as violent and tragic as its first half, but it was just as messy and hampered by the dreadful ache of depression as well as the inevitable letdown after climbing to such a magnificent creative height.

When Nanette says that her father saved his own life by writing *Slaughterhouse-Five*, she suggests that he was able to make life more bearable from an inner suffering caused by his wartime trauma. But she says that her father knew from an early age that "life is trauma," and that art could make it feel better but not that it could wipe out the inevitability of pain.

Just a few weeks after committing himself in the *New York Times* to no longer being clumsy, Vonnegut was awkwardly looming over 23-year-old Mark in an unkempt apartment in Vancouver, Canada, after Mark had experienced a psychotic break while living on a commune. He'd also been doing mescaline. In February 1971, Vonnegut drove Mark to a mental facility and spent a week caring for his son, a role he wasn't accustomed to. In Shields's retelling, Vonnegut was fairly inept.

"Kurt was more like an unpredictable younger brother who refused to grow up than a father," Mark wrote in his second book, *Just Like Someone Without Mental Illness Only More So*. "He was a wonderful writer and capable of great warmth and kindness but he fiercely defended and exercised his right to be a pain in the ass on a regular basis."

Vonnegut fought the impression that his breakup with Jane was the cliché of a struggling writer dumping his wife at the first whiff of success. "Many people regard me as heartless for leaving her," he wrote to a friend. He sent letters to his daughter Nanette, trying to convince her that he wasn't in New York City because he'd run off with another woman. "I wasn't stolen away by another woman," he wrote. "I don't think people can steal other people. I simply went away because the fighting was making everybody so unhappy."

In another letter to Nanette, he wrote, "Terrific depressions are going to crunch me down at regular intervals. . . . Those awful dips still come. We inherited those regular dips."

There were other painful changes. Vonnegut discarded another loyal champion from his past, editor Knox Burger, who had published his first story in 1950. After *Slaughterhouse-Five* came out, Burger switched to being an agent with the understanding that Vonnegut would be his star client. But the author apparently reneged on a promise to follow his old friend.

Vonnegut's marriage with Krementz was also said to be contentious and nearly fell apart. And he continued to have extended bouts of depression, reaching a nadir with his attempted suicide in 1984. Of course, there was also "plain old death," as he wrote in *Slaughterhouse-Five*. Jane died in 1986. Vonnegut watched as his friends and colleagues passed away, such as Bernard V. O'Hare in 1990, one by one.

But from what I can garner from his family and friends, Vonnegut managed to abide by his beloved uncle Alex's quote, "If this isn't nice, I don't know what is." Vonnegut often returned to the quote in his writing and speeches. The point was to recognize and appreciate the good moments in life.

And he continued to write. After 1973's *Breakfast of Champions*, Vonnegut wrote seven more novels up to 1997 and heaps more essays and speeches up to his death. And although none of his writing received close to the acclaim of *Slaughterhouse-Five*, "he was enormously proud of what he did," Mark says. "And he should have been. He often tried to play it off and be humble, but he was not humble. He was incredibly proud of his work."

HAVING PRODUCED the "blossom" that was *Slaughterhouse-Five*, Vonnegut appears to have tried to distance himself from the subject of Dresden in the years since. After the initial publicity rush surrounding the book's publication, Vonnegut began telling interviewers that they were not allowed to ask him about the bombing. He told them he'd written a book about it and that was all he had to say. But he couldn't stop himself. He'd bring it up in those interviews, conversations, speeches, nonfiction writing, and more subtly in some of his later fiction.

In 1976, he was invited to speak at a screening of Marcel Ophuls's *Memory of Justice*, a searing documentary about war crimes and atrocities. He showed up but, after watching the film, went "mum," he says. He simply left.

It seems he was wrestling with himself. In 1976, in a preface of a special edition of *Slaughterhouse-Five*, he wrote, "I, for one, am not avid to keep the memory of the firebombing fresh. I would of course be charmed if people continued to read this book for years to come, but not because I think there are important lessons to be learned from the Dresden catastrophe. I myself was in the midst of it, and learned only that people can become so enraged in war that they will burn great cities to the ground, and slay the inhabitants thereof. That was nothing new." Maybe he was going through a depression when he wrote that. Or he was playing with the dimmer on his dark humor.

In 1981's *Palm Sunday*, Vonnegut claimed to have not given Dresden much thought and repeated his old joke that he was the only person to benefit from the bombing. "Some business I'm in," he wrote.

But then in 1987, after getting through five more novels, Vonnegut's World War II experiences resurfaced in a different, even edifying way in *Bluebeard*. The book's protagonist, Rabo Karabekian, who carries the legacy of the genocide of his Armenian parents' generation, is a veteran of World War II who was

Vonnegut at a talk at Butler University in his hometown of
Indianapolis, Indiana, in 1983.
Photograph by Joe B. McDonald, courtesy of Abby McDonald.

captured by the Nazis during the Battle of the Bulge, just like
Pilgrim and Vonnegut. He also shares their experience of being
released at the end of the war and ending up in an almost mysti-
cal valley filled with survivors of war: refugees, former prisoners,
Holocaust survivors, Gypsies, and German soldiers.

Although he becomes a wealthy painter, Karabekian is alienated and lonely. He has locked up a personal secret, which serves as a symbol of his stunted self, in a potato barn outside his house. By the end of the book, he is compelled to open the barn to reveal himself and his family history: an enormous, hyper-real painting of the World War II valley, which he calls "happy valley." The book ends when the painting is exposed, bestowing upon Karabekian the promise of living a better, more connected life.

Bluebeard stands out as Vonnegut's most positive depiction of the redemptive power of art. But then the author did an about-face in his next book of nonfiction. In 1991's *Fates Worse than Death*, he quotes a speech he had given for the American Psychiatric Association in Philadelphia in 1988: "The firebombing of Dresden explains absolutely nothing about why I write what I write and am what I am. I am sure you are miles ahead of me in thinking of a thousand clinical reasons for this being true. I didn't give a damn about Dresden. I didn't know anybody there." As harsh as this sounds, he did soften his tone by later saying, "I will say anything to be funny, often in the most horrible situations."

Vonnegut also gave a speech at the National Air and Space Museum in Washington, DC, in 1990, in which he went into detail about his experiences during the war and wryly derided the devastating impact of being bombed. But then he asked himself, "Should Dresden have been firebombed?" "No," he responded, dispensing with any hint of Tralfamadorian equivocation.

And then in a prologue to the twenty-fifth anniversary edition of *Slaughterhouse-Five* in 1994, he wrote, "I have no regrets about this book. . . . It is a nonjudgmental expression of astonishment at what I saw and did in Dresden after it was firebombed."

He also mentions a moral imperative that guided his writing of it: "The inhumanity of many of man's inventions to man," he said. "That is the dominant theme of what I have written during the past forty-five years or so."

It appears that in the four decades after he wrote *Slaughterhouse-Five*, Vonnegut displayed everything from indifference to indignation to resignation to astonishment and even to hope when he revisited his experiences during the war. And he physically returned to Dresden in 1998; trailed by a film crew while he took deep, swift drags on his Pall Malls, he walked solemnly through the slaughterhouse where he had been imprisoned fifty years earlier. "Only then did I realize that we had seen an Atlantis—before it sank forever beneath the waves," he wrote in a letter to Loree Rackstraw (originally Wilson), his onetime "beautiful trouble" with whom he had maintained a close epistolary relationship. He also gave a talk and shared this thought with Rackstraw about his German audience; "I have seen Dresden, and you have not," he wrote.

Another reckoning occurred earlier, in 1995, when Vonnegut went to do a speech in Rochester, New York, where Joe Crone, the real-life Billy Pilgrim, had lived. The author had found out that both of Crone's parents had passed away, so he felt free to tell a local journalist about his inspiration, after keeping it secret for twenty-five years. The trip turned out to be more of a reconciliation with his past than Vonnegut had counted on. Upon his arrival, his hosts asked him if he wanted to visit Crone's grave, which shocked him, because Vonnegut thought Crone was still buried in Dresden.

But unbeknownst to Vonnegut, Crone's parents had found their son's burial site and, with the help of the East German government, had had his body exhumed and reburied in Rochester. Vonnegut's hosts brought him to the cemetery, where he approached the grave alone. Vonnegut had a solemn, solitary smoke standing over Crone's headstone. When he returned to the car, he said, "Well, that closes the book on World War II for me."

CHAPTER THIRTEEN

SLAUGHTERHOUSE-FIVE'S PLACE IN HISTORY (DESPITE THAT WHOLE TIMELESSNESS THING)

"THE STORY of the senselessness of war needs to be told afresh in every generation for it to be heard," author Matthew Thomas said in a review of Iraq War veteran Phil Klay's celebrated 2014 book of short stories, *Redeployment*. "We think we know war stories, and he makes us see that we don't know *these* war stories," Thomas wrote.

Klay, who took the New York University Veterans Writing Workshop, which preceded the Words After War workshop, with Matt Gallagher and Matthew Mellina in 2010, agrees with Thomas's assessment. He is wary of a tendency toward believing that "there's a particular message that a war story is going to tell you and that once you have received that message, you know, you can dispose of it," Klay tells me over the phone. "Like, 'Oh, I read [Wilfred Owen's] *Dulce et Decorum Est*, now I know that it is not particularly pleasant to die in war. Now I don't need to read any more war literature.'"

"You're always going to need new books that respond to the moment," says Klay, who won the National Book Award for *Redeployment* after being deployed in Anbar Province from 2007 to 2008 as a public affairs officer for the US Marines. He didn't see any combat—"only its aftermath," he says. Klay has since written a novel, *Missionaries*, and now teaches writing at Fairfield University. In the 2010 NYU group, it was clear that Klay "had 'it,' " according to Gallagher. "It's no surprise to anyone that he has been wildly successful as a writer."

Wars tend to impact the different generations that fight them differently, and that includes more than the details of engagements and death tolls, although both are significant. There is a complex confluence of other forces affecting each generation, including the prevailing culture, the moral and political justification of the war, whether or not there's a draft, the new technology of warfare and war medicine, the homecoming realities, and so on—all of which make the soldiers' experience of that war unique.

This doesn't mean that there aren't similarities or that the wisdom and insight of previous generations of war writers doesn't apply. As Tim O'Brien says to me, "I don't think that we should dismiss Tolstoy." In Vietnam, O'Brien was buoyed by the works of Hemingway and other writers. "Surely *War and Peace*, the *Iliad*, *A Farewell to Arms*, *The Red Badge of Courage*, and many other books and poems still resonate across the generations," he says.

They do. But Klay is also correct when he says, "We tend to forget the lessons of war over and over again."

Part of what made *Slaughterhouse-Five* so "afresh," as it were, was that it spoke so directly to two war generations—World War II and Vietnam—giving it timelessness and therefore Great Book importance. (And, actually, make that three wars: I'll commit the cliché of folding Korea into World War II.) The best war books are often measured by their staying power or their ability to speak to and for a generation. The great ones, such as *Slaughterhouse-Five*, do both.

And from the writers' perspective, the need for new stories and the resilience of old ones influences how they process war and, more precisely, *their* wars. They write for their generations and also respond to the work of previous writers, creating a circular but also evolving literary tradition.

Klay and I talk about how Vonnegut and Joseph Heller wrote their great war books in response to Mailer's *The Naked and the Dead*, "which comes out pretty quickly right after World War II and it's a more straightforward model in many ways," Klay says. "Joseph Heller read *The Naked and the Dead* and just gave up on what he was writing. He realized he needed to find a new way of talking. Both Heller and Vonnegut spent years not just trying to figure out a way around their experiences but also finding a form suitable for the difficult subject. What is possible to bring a reader along, such that they feel that they're not being given a dispatch from hell that they view at a distance, but are being ushered inside a world that is telling them difficult truths, and also where they actually want to continue to dwell for the time inside that book?"

Woven into the fabric of *Slaughterhouse-Five* is that it is a response. Vonnegut took Mary O'Hare's admonition to not write a book that could star John Wayne or Frank Sinatra as his mandate to write something different from what had been done before. But it's also hard to imagine *Slaughterhouse-Five* without *Catch-22* having been published eight years earlier. Or without Stanley Kubrick's *Dr. Strangelove or: How I Learned to Stop Worrying and Love the Bomb* appearing in theaters in 1964. Vonnegut had two stellar, absurdist precedents.

Vonnegut deftly honored his literary past in *Slaughterhouse-Five*. For instance, he made clear allusions to Herman Melville's *Moby-Dick*, the story driven by the post-traumatic experiences of Captain Ahab, who hunts down the whale that bit off his leg. "The central image of post-traumatic stress is that of Ishmael at the end of *Moby-Dick*, floating atop Queequeg's coffin, looking out over the vastness of the sea," Duke psychiatrist Harold Kudler tells David Morris for his book *The Evil Hours*.

Vonnegut puts Billy Pilgrim on a coffin-shaped wagon at the end of *Slaughterhouse-Five*. Pilgrim is also paired up on the last pages of the book with a dead ringer for the tattooed Queequeg: a Maori soldier (strange: How did he end up with an American POW detail in Germany in 1945?) with a face covered in tattoos of whirlpools (Ahab and the *Pequod* crew are sucked into a whirlpool created by Moby-Dick), who dies from the dry heaves while cleaning up bodies in Dresden.

Vonnegut joins Melville on the precipice, both authors looking into the same existential abyss that haunts human existence. And they do it with characters struggling with trauma. "It is after the tempest," Dr. Kudler says to me, "this coming out on the other end of the maelstrom with your mortality intact. Somehow you came out alive and you got to this point in this crazy world and view what's behind you and in front of you."

In an interview in 1987 with National Public Radio's Terry Gross, Vonnegut used dialectical terms to explain *Slaughterhouse-Five*: "My own feeling is that civilization ended in World War I, and we're still trying to recover from that. Much of the blame is the malarkey that artists have created to glorify war, which, as we all know, is nonsense, and a good deal worse than that—romantic pictures of battle, and of the dead and men in uniform and all that. And I did not want to have that story told again."

As true as it is about what Vonnegut said about World War I—that it was a devastating turning point in human history—it is not incidental that that tragic conflict was also the primary factor in his parents' long decline. Vonnegut was trying to reclaim civilization for all of us, but also to restore the dignity that his own family lost because of World War I.

Every war leaves a rippling legacy of devastation that a new generation of writers has tried to process, trying to reclaim civilization. Look no further than F. Scott Fitzgerald's great American novel, *The Great Gatsby*, the story of Jay Gatsby and Nick Carraway, about two World War I veterans unable to reconcile with their pasts.

Dr. Kudler and Professor Karen English both make strong cases with me that Fitzgerald's two *Gatsby* protagonists experienced trauma in the war. Gatsby, a man who lies about his war experiences, tries to reinvent himself and ultimately fails. "You can't repeat the past," Carraway says to him. To which Gatsby responds, "Why of course you can!"

"Modern readers usually regard *Gatsby* as a tale of the jazz age but Fitzgerald's contemporaries had a better chance of recognizing Gatsby and Carraway as members of the Lost Generation of WW I veterans," Dr. Kudler said in a talk he gave in 2010. "Fitzgerald imagines a man who tries to harness that posttraumatic malleability of self, society, and even time for his own purposes."

Another example is the work of J. D. Salinger, who, like Fitzgerald, didn't experience combat as a soldier, but as a member of the Counter Intelligence Corps during World War II he interviewed POWs and went to at least one concentration camp. Salinger was sent to a hospital for combat fatigue during the war, and although he didn't speak about being traumatized, many of his stories include veterans mentally crippled by their war experiences, most notably, "A Perfect Day for Bananafish," about a shattered GI who takes his own life. Vonnegut and Salinger, who came from an era known for quiet fortitude, gave voice to the disquieting realities of war. Vonnegut was born at the tail end of the Greatest Generation, close to the beginning of the Silent Generation; the former prided themselves for enduring great hardship and persevering, while the latter, which he appears to have identified with more, were given their generational label in a *Time* magazine article for not asserting themselves, which Vonnegut dismissed as "supreme irony," having just won a world war.

Audie Murphy, the most decorated American soldier of World War II, whose remarkably heroic acts in battle were made into the movie *To Hell and Back*, personifies the repression that underlies that era. He was given parades and magazine covers, but few Americans knew that their hero also suffered from debilitating war trauma. He developed a nervous condition, couldn't sleep, had fits of violence, and became addicted to pharmaceuticals. But the language, the science, and the cultural reference points hadn't yet been created to allow his trauma to be expressed or heard.

"They took Army dogs and rehabilitated them for civilian life," Murphy said in 1960. "But they turned soldiers into civilians immediately and let 'em sink or swim."

When he was once asked how soldiers manage to survive a war, he replied, "I don't think they ever do."

Although Murphy spoke openly about the damage the war had done to him, that difficult part of his story didn't find traction with the Silent Generation, which goes some way toward framing why Vonnegut refused to acknowledge the impact of the war on himself. Yes, he eventually broke the silence by writing about the bombing of Dresden and creating traumatized fictional characters, but he roundly denied the war's impact on him personally.

"The denial is astounding," says Vietnam veteran and author Karl Marlantes, who has been outspoken about his own struggle with PTSD. He isn't talking specifically about Vonnegut but more generally about the World War II veterans who have confronted him about PTSD. "They'd say, 'We don't have any of this post-traumatic stress disorder bullshit. We didn't have any of that,'" Marlantes says with mock exasperation. "To which I'd say, 'No, but you had three-martini lunches and you couldn't go home after work until you'd had three more.'"

Marlantes, who grew up in Oregon and passed on a Rhodes Scholarship at Oxford to serve as a marine lieutenant during some of the worst fighting in Vietnam from 1968 to 1969, had a long journey like Vonnegut to finally publishing his war novel, 2010's *Matterhorn*. But he took a very different emotional path.

After the war, while he tried to write a novel about his experiences, Marlantes became a successful businessman. But, haunted by his memories of combat, he began to act erratically. "I still have PTSD but if I was talking about this subject like this twenty-five years ago, I would be trembling," he tells me over the phone.

Marlantes confronted his problem. He went to group therapy sessions at the VA. He accepted his PTSD diagnosis. He also embraced a spiritual path to combat his demons. And, eventually, his writing got published. *Matterhorn*, which is in the realist tradition of a Hemingway novel, is not clearly an anti-war book, but that doesn't make it a pro-war book either. Marlantes sees his own writing as a next step after *Slaughterhouse-Five*, particularly his willingness to write about what he considers to be the redemptive aspects of combat. As noted earlier, Marlantes differs from Vonnegut and O'Brien in including in his writing the notion that war contains elements that are appealing, such as the camaraderie between soldiers, the excitement of shooting guns, and the ironically life-affirming experience of almost dying.

"Look at how fascinated we are by war," Marlantes says, "Was Kurt Vonnegut not being honest? He was writing at a time when you could not say something like that. I'll make up a theory that Kurt Vonnegut was of the generation that had to dispel the bugles. The next step is the next generation, which is me. And it might be 'You know, it might be a little bit of each.'

"If you deny it, you are not being completely honest," he says. "I use the analogy of crack cocaine. If you tell kids that crack won't make you feel good, you are lying to them. But then you tell them that they will have to pay the price for that high."

Also noted earlier: O'Brien is wary of where this line of thinking could lead "I find it offensive and I find it wrong—factually, wrong," he says. "I don't think war makes you a better person."

This is the ebb and flow of ideas about war and war writing that can occur within and between generations. Another example: Pretty much every veteran writer I spoke with, including Marlantes, reveres the work of the Great War poets, but the likes of Owen, Sassoon, and others had at least one harsh critic. In 1936, W. B. Yeats edited *The Oxford Book of Modern Verse* and excluded all of those who had given voice to the trauma of World War I. His reasoning: "Passive suffering is not a theme for poetry," he sniffed.

NEW YORKER MAGAZINE writer and bestselling author Malcolm Gladwell took a crack at distilling how different generations cope with war trauma through literature in 2004 when he wrote an article, "Getting Over It," that challenged the prevailing wisdom about the durable effects of trauma. The *New Yorker* article's premise was that maybe the current dominant belief that trauma should have long-term effects on a person isn't accurate and that, in fact, we could learn from a previous generation to just move on.

Gladwell uses Sloan Wilson's popular 1955 novel, *The Man in the Gray Flannel Suit*, to demonstrate that trauma need not be so, well, traumatizing. The protagonist, Tom Rath, has terrible experiences during World War II, which he suppresses with alcohol and denial. But in Gladwell's interpretation, he gets over it by the end of the novel.

Gladwell quotes Rath's thinking about his violent memories of World War II: "All these facts were simply incomprehensible and had to be forgotten. That, he had decided, was the final truth of the war, and he had greeted it with relief, greeted it eagerly, the simple fact that it was incomprehensible and had to be forgotten. Things just happen, he had decided; they happen and they happen again, and anybody who tries to make sense out of it goes out of his mind."

Gladwell doesn't see this as unhealthy repression. He takes it at face value. And Gladwell appreciates how Rath's trauma "does not destroy him, or leave him permanently traumatized."

He contrasts Wilson's book with Tim O'Brien's 1994 novel, *In the Lake of the Woods*, which is about a Vietnam veteran who is unable to shake his war demons and is overwhelmed by them. "Somehow in the intervening decades our understanding of what it means to experience a traumatic event has changed," Gladwell writes. "It's worth wondering whether we've got it right."

Before I go on, I don't think Gladwell got Wilson's book right. Although *The Man in the Gray Flannel Suit* ends with Rath seemingly moving forward after he reconciles with his infidelity during the war, he's hardly a model of redemption. He is still a vessel, a man in a suit, and a raging alcoholic with a haunted war past to boot. Unlike Gladwell, I don't think his restoration is assured.

The consensus takeaway of the book has always been that Rath is a stand-in for a generation that has become hollow—organization men, and their domesticated wives, who are little more than the clothes they fit into. Gladwell applauds an unearned hopeful ending to a book that most people consider to be a critique of a generation.

Gladwell then uses a 1998 study that was published in *Psychological Bulletin* to drive a wedge between the Wilson and O'Brien novels. The study, which analyzed fifty-nine other studies on long-term psychological effects of childhood sexual abuse, indicated that trauma survivors had only marginally more problems later in life than those without a history of abuse.

Gladwell embraces this finding as evidence of the "resilience of the human spirit," but he does a lot of his own damage along the way. First, despite it being potentially good news that a number of trauma survivors don't have long-term problems, what does that mean for those who do? They're still there. They're still living with long-term problems from their trauma. They still deserve our sympathy and attention and to be given the treatment to cope with their trauma. Gladwell's article suggests that, well, maybe they, too, should be "getting over it."

He makes the exception that people with really bad trauma have a harder time getting over it. But doesn't that exception prove that his entire argument—that maybe we should just get over it—is flawed? Or is he just saying that, in some more minor instances of trauma, those people should, on average, be able to move on?

OK, but the implications are boorish. And his research is flawed. In addition to the aforementioned study, he refers to only one other, about losing a spouse. But the article is centered on Rath's war experiences and therefore about a totally different form of trauma. All traumas can't be treated equally.

There's implicit judgment by Gladwell of O'Brien's character and anyone who carries their trauma with them. *What's the matter with you?* he seems to say. *Can't you see that you're a part of a larger cultural trend?*

Gladwell's take—the subtitle of his story is "The Man in the Gray Flannel Suit put the war behind him. Why can't we?"—may be more refined, but it is as reactionary as General George S. Patton's slap in the head.

The notion that it's terribly hard to put the pieces back together again after war has become so accepted that it looms, to someone like Gladwell, like a piñata ripe for a takedown. But as smart as it is to question any orthodoxy, the counternarrative can be just as prone to assumptions and lazy thinking as that which it counters. By narrowing his approach to his interpretation of one book, and then generalizing it, and then applying a couple of tenuously related studies to his thesis, Gladwell makes a weak case. This is even more glaring in light of the new science on trauma. Never mind the hype caused by an Ariana Grande brain scan. She was actually pointing to real science. There is plenty of hard scientific evidence that shows that there is a biological impact from PTSD on the brain as well as alterations to other physiological systems.

It is also dubious how Gladwell takes one book to represent the wisdom from the past. You could just as well find literature from that same past, such as Salinger's stories, *The Great Gatsby*, or *Slaughterhouse-Five*, that supports a contrary thesis that, in fact, veterans can't "just put the war behind them."

HOWEVER FLAWED Gladwell's article may be, it is a welcome attempt at looking at the historical, often cyclical back-and-forth relationship between literature, war trauma, and science that continues into the twenty-first century. Today, Iraq and Afghanistan veteran writers come of age with access to a clinical understanding of their possible traumas, the support of writing workshops, and a culture primed to put a PTSD stamp on their inner struggles to express themselves.

While Vonnegut mostly churned out his war story alone, tapping away on his typewriter in Barnstable or Iowa, Klay and Mellina and Gallagher and other like-minded veterans gathered for the New York University Veterans Writing Workshop, meeting at a town house in Greenwich Village once a week from September to May in 2010 to sit on lounge chairs under photographs of famous writers that included Vonnegut as well as Mailer, James Baldwin, Saul Bellow, and other literary luminaries.

Guided by NYU creative writing graduate students, the veterans reviewed each other's writing. "It was a kinda halfway house for soldiers and new veterans trying to become comfortable with our civilian skins and writer identities at the same time," Gallagher says. After going through writing exercises and giving notes on each other's work, a scrum of the vets would continue the discussion or argue politics and philosophy at the Half Pint bar or the White Horse Tavern, where Mailer, Jack Kerouac and other writers once drank.

"It's extremely helpful to have a bunch of guys and gals who are working through similar issues in different ways," Klay says. "I still try and work with a lot of these folks. And the collective output informs me."

Gallagher says that they were happy to be out of the military and to be with each other to talk about literature and share their work. There was "a cohesion that came from this crazy belief that this subject mattered, which was not then a known thing," he says. "There was an open question about whether this stuff was going to find a wider audience. It wasn't accepted wisdom back in 2010. This was pre–*Billy Lynn's Long Halftime Walk* [non-veteran author Ben Fountain's 2012 bestselling novel about a stateside public relations tour by a unit of Iraq War soldiers], pre–*Yellow Birds*."

Gallagher says that the group admired the commercial success of 2003's *Jarhead*, Anthony Swofford's book about fighting in the Persian Gulf War, but even if it was a "powerfully voice-driven memoir," according to Gallagher, "it wasn't like anyone was saying, 'I want to write the new *Jarhead*.'" In Iraq, his unit would joke about Swofford's war, a one-hundred-hour engagement. "We used to say, 'I had patrols that lasted that long,'" Gallagher admits.

"And, you know, looking back on that, that's kind of punkish and self-satisfied." (It's also military tradition; I once heard of a World War II vet who joined a group of Vietnam vets at a VA therapy group and said, "Vietnam was a brushfire [compared to WW II].") Gallagher and his peers found more inspiration in earlier wars and the literary output and personages of the Great War poets, along with James Salter, Crane, Hemingway, O'Brien, Vonnegut, Heller, and Mailer ("without the wife stabbing"). "These were the writers we wanted to be like," Gallagher says.

More workshops, such as the Veterans Writing Project in Washington, DC, and the Writers Guild Foundation's Veterans Writing Project in Los Angeles, served veterans across the country. And further support came from *New York Times* editor Peter Catapano, who had a literature, as opposed to journalism, background and who began an online series in which he hoped to "track the homecoming experience of veterans, their readjustment to civilian life and family issues," he says.

Catapano called the series "Home Fires" and started it in 2010 with a five-part memoir by Iraq War veteran Roy Scranton, who wrote about the confusion and frustration of returning home from fighting a war while his fellow self-involved generation of Americans obsessed over quirky dinner parties and played kickball well into their thirties. "I was getting a sense that these writers were shaping up to be a literary generation," Catapano says. The series ultimately ran more than one hundred articles by dozens of veterans. "The talent pool was super high and their sense of history and war literature was part of what they were doing."

Catapano was asked to help curate veteran readings at the Old Stone House in Brooklyn, where some of his "Home Fires"

Matt Gallagher served in Iraq for fifteen months, beginning in 2007,
as an armored cavalry officer. Courtesy of Matt Gallagher.

writers, such as Scranton, Gallagher, and Klay, read from their
work. Scranton and Gallagher also co-edited a book of short
material, 2013's *Fire and Forget*, dubbed "an impressive anthology," by the *New York Times*, and that included work by many of
their workshop peers.

"The writing was a way for them to remake themselves as citizens of their country," Catapano says. "It's finding a path in life after you've served. They want to be the witnesses to what went on over there."

Catapano casts this new generation in terms quite similar to how Vonnegut perceived himself. "I was hoping to build a country and add to its literature," Vonnegut said later in life. "That's why I served in World War II, and that's why I wrote books."

But Vonnegut's voice was a rare one coming from a mostly silent generation. His struggle to write his story was something he kept mostly to himself, whereas Klay struggled openly about writing in front of his peers, and millions of other readers, in the *New York Times*, as he did in a piece in 2010. "The telling tends to decay into a kind of pornographic, voyeuristic experience," he wrote. "I feel I do disservice to the enormity of my subject by making it a subject of conversation. And yet I know that keeping a hushed silence is a failure, too, because by not telling these stories we fail to process them."

To the best of my knowledge, Vonnegut never sat in a room with a VA-organized group of veterans to process his feelings. Nor did he ever workshop drafts of his novel with soldiers from World War II. He suffered the silence of the Silent Generation. Having failed to recall the bombing of Dresden, what he did do was try to talk with his fellow slaughterhouse POWs about their memories. "They didn't remember, either," he said in an interview. "They didn't want to talk about it."

These are some considerable differences between his experience and those of today's generation of young veterans. Gallagher emphasizes that there is another, even more fundamental one: Today's soldier belongs to an all-volunteer army. Without the draft, Gallagher says that there is a greater "ambiguity" about a veteran writer's denunciation of the war he or she signed up for. "There's a cautious realism there," he says. "I fear we've been overly concerned with political realism. And that clarity and power that can come with philosophical truth has suffered as a result. In a lot of O'Brien's work, he does none of that throat clearing. He's just very straightforward about his pacifism. And that certainly applies to Vonnegut's work as well."

Gallagher, who has continued to teach the Words After War workshop, which is also affiliated with NYU, waited in a line in 2010 to get a book signed by O'Brien at a twentieth-anniversary event for *The Things They Carried* at a Barnes & Noble bookstore in Manhattan. He pursued O'Brien until the two veteran writers eventually got to know each other in 2019 at the prestigious Sewanee Writers' Conference in Tennessee. O'Brien now considers Gallagher a friend, one he is enthusiastic about supporting as a writer. "The fact that he can come up with thoughts about the absence of moral clarity means he's got some moral clarity," O'Brien says with a laugh.

Gallagher's first novel, *Youngblood*, is a story of an American lieutenant in Iraq confronted by a moral quandary and romantic mystery. His second, *Empire City*, takes place in a futuristic, alternate reality. Both received positive reviews. "I keep saying I'm done with writing war stories, but I'm doing it again," he says of his next novel. "War is bad. We all know that, right? But how do you make that a compelling story with moral heft?"

BEFORE THE SUN ROSE the February morning we first spoke on the phone, Tim O'Brien was doing dishes in his home in Austin,

Texas. He was thinking about *The Things They Carried*, which he wrote thirty years ago, and how it no longer belongs to him. "I feel divorced from my book," he told me later that day. "The book is there on the shelf and it's not mine anymore. It once was when I was writing it. But I don't remember writing the sentences or the words or taking this or that clause out. A book starts to belong less and less to the author and more and more to the world."

O'Brien reminds me that it's delicate and dicey writing about the relationship between a book and its author or the era it comes from. "I don't think any writer is ever comfortable with any declaration about a book that he or she has written," he says. "Especially when you can't declare it to yourself. How can someone else know what it is you wrote if you don't?"

"My books are in some ways mysteries to me," he adds.

But that's how it should be. As much as I've tried to pull out the threads on *Slaughterhouse-Five* to determine its relationship to war trauma, a book can never be just one thing. That includes what its author intended or the year it came out. It also often includes its genre: The best war novels aren't just about war.

As it turns out, a warped sense of time and a splintered sense of self does more than describe the impact of war; it also provides a pretty good primer on life in the twenty-first century. "Vonnegut is getting more and more astute in diagnosing the American pathologies that are getting worse and worse and yet he's doing it from a greater remove," says writer Steve Almond. "It's right there in front of us. We have these powerful devices and screens that disembody us and take us out of the place and also out of the present. You can be in your house right next to somebody and they are somewhere else."

"*Slaughterhouse-Five* can be seen as a parable of the divided self," he concludes. "We are constantly in more than one place at one time, shuttling around in time and space. And that disrupts a coherent, singular narrative where we can know ourselves. We are off fleeing the chaos of our inner lives."

Many writers agree. There is a long list of authors who consider Vonnegut to be a seminal influence, including John Irving, John Green, Dave Eggers, Rick Moody, and Jonathan Safran Foer, each of whom has written about the splintering effects of pain. When Ismet Prcic, a Bosnian Muslim whose family was torn apart by the Balkan wars of the 1990s, came to America, he read *Slaughterhouse-Five* and recognized that "it captured something I was feeling but didn't know how to express yet."

Prcic says his 2011 novel, *Shards*, was heavily influenced by Vonnegut. As the title indicates, Prcic sees the world and his past in fragments—discontinuous pieces that were scattered by his traumatic adolescence.

"You have a life, a family, a country, a set of moral rules that you grow up with. And then war starts, and everything is gone. All those agreements, like you shouldn't kill people, you shouldn't separate family members from their family, goes to shit," he says. "You look at the snapshots of your life and you can't see a continuity."

By splintering reality, time, memory, and Pilgrim's identity, Vonnegut aestheticized one of the primary effects of trauma, dissociation, in which there is a disconnection or lack of continuity between one's thoughts. "Normal, nontraumatic memories are owned and integrated into the ongoing story of the self," David Morris writes in *The Evil Hours*. "In contrast, the traumatic memory stands apart, like a feral dog, snarling, wild, and unpredictable."

But it's not just the clinically diagnosed traumatized person that Vonnegut depicted. Almond notes that Vonnegut was very concerned with our "big brains," and how our innovations in science and technology could endanger all of us. Vonnegut passed away before our smartphones and social media became the mediums through which we see ourselves, literally and figuratively, but check this out: Reliving the experience (flashback), avoiding the event, having negative thoughts, experiencing hyperarousal, having troubled sleep, blaming self or others, social withdrawal, loss of memory—all of the attributes of PTSD could easily describe my sixteen-year-old daughter's daily intake of Instagram.

No wonder PTSD has become a signature mental disorder of our age. There is more than mere correlation happening here: If there are similar attributes to being glued to a screen and to experiencing PTSD, then they will reinforce each other in individuals and the culture at large. There is a symbiotic relationship.

What I find remarkable about *Slaughterhouse-Five* is that Vonnegut used his insight, observational powers, and narrative skills to convey the impact of war trauma, and then the book takes a life of its own and transcends its place in history by anticipating the PTSD diagnosis. But it doesn't do it by magic or time travel. It is because Vonnegut captures the delicate relationship between the human condition, pain, memory, and time. By doing this, he tells us who we are and he deciphers how our culture is changing.

PTSD is, after all, a "product of culture as much as a hardwired biological fact," writes David Morris, who references Otto

Fenichel, one of the pioneers of modern psychology, who wrote that neuroses, or what we'd now call mental disorders, are not a physical inevitability like aging; they emerge within a context. "Neuroses are social diseases," he wrote, "corresponding to a given and historically developed social milieu. They cannot be changed without corresponding change in the milieu."

Vonnegut was a part of that change. PTSD can be construed as an "invention," according to McGill University's Allan Young, a medical anthropologist. This is not to say that it isn't real, but, as quoted in Morris's *Evil Hours*, "the disorder is not timeless, nor does it possess an intrinsic unity. Rather, it is glued together by the practices, technologies, and narratives with which it is diagnosed, studied, treated, and represented and by the various interests, institutions, and moral arguments that mobilized these efforts and resources."

For example, Morris pinpoints the development of the flashback symptom, the telltale sign of PTSD. He finds the roots in the dawn of the moving image. Early twentieth-century filmmakers coined the term *flashback* to refer to a jump backwards within a movie. And according to London's King's College researchers, flashbacks were nearly nonexistent among soldiers who fought before the age of film. Morris notes that Civil War veterans tended to describe their involuntary episodes of mental images, of "seeing things," as phantasmic visitations. Those were the days when people attempted to speak to the dead through seances. Now we settle with looking at a deceased person's Twitter feed.

"It is tempting to wonder if film, television, and increasingly, video games don't provide the lion's share of our modern traumatic vocabulary," Morris writes. "Teaching us how to see our memories in the way that photography taught us how to see (and not see) sunsets."

Vonnegut poked at the deep connection between cinema, trauma, and memory in *Slaughterhouse-Five*, on the night that Pilgrim is abducted by the Tralfamadorians, when he watches a war movie on television and becomes unstuck. Pilgrim watches the movie backwards so that American bomber pilots fly their planes backwards from an English airstrip, backwards over Germany, where their bombs are returned to their bays and the fires below are extinguished and the bombs are returned to the factories where they are dismantled and the American soldiers are returned to being fresh-faced high school kids.

It's such a poignant, elemental, and entirely relatable sequence, one that may not have been entirely original—science fiction writer Philip K. Dick had implemented a similar device in his 1967 novel, *Counter-Clock World*, which was based on his short story "Your Appointment Will Be Yesterday," and there are other reverse-chronology examples in literature dating back to the *Aeneid*—but in the context of Billy Pilgrim's disassembling mental state is nonetheless particularly touching. Enough so that author Martin Amis was later inspired by Vonnegut to write his 1991 novel about the Holocaust, *Time's Arrow*, in reverse. And director Ken Burns confirms with me that he got the idea from *Slaughterhouse-Five* to open his 2017 *The Vietnam War* documentary series with a similar depiction of the war being turned back on itself.

It is a widely beloved moment in the book. I was most moved by the story that Fred Greybar, a former marine and Chicago suburban native who fought in Vietnam in 1968, told me. I met Greybar in Indianapolis fifty years to the day that he flew out of Da Nang, after serving in a war that he knew then "the guys we were fighting were more in the right than we were." With tears in his eyes, he recalled his father having warned him before he enlisted that "in six months you are going to be sitting in a swamp with a gun in your hand and not wanting to be anywhere near there," Greybar said. "He was off by four months."

After Greybar came home from Vietnam, he was deeply confused by what he had just experienced. He appreciated how his parents pushed him to put the war behind him by going back to college while he worked a night shift as a machinist. He was assigned to read *Slaughterhouse-Five* for a class. One night while on a break at work, he took the novel to read in a bathroom stall. He read the scene of Billy Pilgrim's war movie being reversed— and, by extension, imagined everything he had just experienced in Vietnam also being erased—and wept an unstoppable stream of tears there on the john.

CHAPTER FOURTEEN
ONE LAST JOKE

IF YOU ASK TIM O'BRIEN, there's no such thing as closure when it comes to war, nor should there be. And if you asked Vonnegut the right way, despite what he said at Joe Crone's grave, I bet he would agree—even if he hid his reply in a joke.

As for the book on Vonnegut, that can also never be closed. And I'd say that the prospect that he had war trauma, which some call PTSD, is a reasonable attempt to write him into a recognizable narrative arc—which is fine up to a point, but I am more comfortable leaving that open. The closest I came to a definitive reveal that Vonnegut was afflicted by his war experiences came from Vonnegut scholar Marc Leeds, who casually said to me, "Well, of course there were the four lines above that first line of the draft that he crossed out in blue ink. Had he left them in, from the very first sentence, everyone would have read it as PTSD."

I felt a twinge in my left eye as he spoke. How could I have missed that? Which version was it? Leeds wasn't sure. He referred me to Professor Jarvis, whom he credited as being a greater authority on the Lilly Library manuscripts. After combing through my thousand-plus photos I'd taken of the Vonnegut records at the Lilly, I got in touch with Jarvis and asked her if she knew of what Leeds spoke. She dove into her files and spent hours looking through the pages. But she couldn't find anything that screamed "PTSD!" any more than any of the discards I've already mentioned here or, actually, what ended up in the final book.

"I think Marc is probably referring to all the times Kurt emphasized the role of his own lived experiences in drafts," she wrote me in an email. "Especially when those moments appeared near scenes of obvious trauma. It's easy to fill in the gaps."

"Nope," Leeds told me. "It's there." But where? He said he took a photo of the draft but it was stored on a flash drive somewhere. He said he'd look for it. He never got back to me.

Speaking of uncertain tales, I don't think that the *Kurt Vonnegut, Nazi Slayer!* storyline has earned its place in the nonfiction section. I would rather call it "speculative fiction," the term used for stories that aren't representations of reality but are related to it through science fiction, fantasy, and alternative reality storytelling. I couldn't find any more evidence to substantiate Kachmar's incredible tale. I just kept thinking of the opposite. In Vonnegut's last novel-cum-memoir, *Timequake*, he says he never shot anyone. And then he jokes that when his uncle Dan told him, "You're a man now," after returning from the war, Vonnegut said, "Damn near killed my first German."

Vonnegut's only crime that I could find, if you can even call it that, was that a conventional revenge tale may have had some appeal for him. In 1954, he wrote a letter to Knox Burger in which he mentioned how much he was affected emotionally by the fall of Dien Bien Phu, a deadly and decisive battle when the communist Viet Minh defeated the French. This was before the United States' protracted war there. In the letter, Vonnegut admitted to being "full of all kinds of primitive feelings—one being that that's the way to go; another being that I wouldn't mind too much getting into a rifle and grenade fight in some clean, dry, sunny place near a first-class hospital."

Or, in 1991's *Fates Worse than Death*, he writes, "As for my pacifism, it is nothing if not ambivalent. When I ask myself what person in American history I would most like to have been, I am powerless to protest when my subconscious nominates Joshua Chamberlain. Colonel Chamberlain, while in command of the 20th Maine Volunteers during the Civil War, ordered a downhill and then uphill bayonet charge which turned the tide of battle in favor of the Union forces at Gettysburg."

These admissions speak to Vonnegut's complex, sometimes contradictory relationship to his ideals, which he addressed in *Palm Sunday*. "The beliefs I have to defend are so soft and complicated, actually, and, when vivisected, turn into bowls of undifferentiated mush. I am a pacifist, I am an anarchist, I am a planetary citizen, and so on," he wrote.

We err when we try to pin him down. When I was visiting Indiana University, I met a very congenial, intelligent author-professor who adored Vonnegut and claimed a sort of kinship with him. We were having drinks with other academics who were talking about the *John Wick* series of films that star Keanu Reeves, and this professor knowingly assured the group that Vonnegut was not a fan of guns. And although it's true that in *Slaughterhouse-Five* Vonnegut says he let his father's guns "rust," I found several unpublished references to his love of shooting and his pride in his marksmanship. There was even a letter from the 1980s to Vonnegut from Wyoming Republican senator Alan Simpson, who fondly remembered the days when the two men enjoyed shooting together and "cutting down a damned three-inch Aspen tree with several boxes of .22 shells." Who would have thought?

"So," you say. "He enjoyed shooting guns. So what? You were talking about killing Nazis in cold blood!" Right, right. I'm simply pointing out that we often get Vonnegut wrong. *Kurt Vonnegut, Nazi Slayer!* was a McGuffin of sorts, my way to begin looking at perception, trauma, and storytelling. I also wanted to remind you that I was here, writing the words on these pages, bringing all my baggage to this book about another man's baggage and book.

I should add that by the time I got to look at war through the eyes of Lance Miccio and Matthew Mellina, it became much less theoretical and entertaining. Not that I know war now. But it's certainly less two-dimensional thanks to two veterans who've been scarred by it. I can't help but feel that there is some of Vonnegut in both of them. They're storytellers who've been to a dark place. And I'm still rooting for Mellina to write his way out of there.

The mystery at the heart of this book isn't whether or not Vonnegut committed a war crime or even if he had PTSD but how he was able to craft *Slaughterhouse-Five*. And I'm never going to solve that one, at least not completely.

But, God bless Mr. Vonnegut, deficiency was central to his narrative approach to Dresden. He proposed in that first chapter that it is the act itself—just like Lot's wife turning to salt when she looks back at Sodom and Gomorrah—that matters. So, in coming up short on Vonnegut, I find solace in Vonnegut! It's just like him to make me feel better.

IT IS UNFORTUNATE THAT, outside of what Vonnegut wrote himself, which anyone who is interested in him should read first, the most complete word on his life and career remains 2011's *And So It Goes* by Charles Shields, who met with his subject two times at the end of his life—the second being the morning of the day he fell down the stairs—and he found him to be a "disenchanted, angry adolescent," casting Vonnegut in a permanently gloomy light.

Of course, Vonnegut earned it. He *was* gloomy. Soon after *Slaughterhouse-Five* came out, reflecting on the "bone-deep sadness" of his parents, Vonnegut said, "After I'm gone, I don't want my children to have to say about me what I have to say about my father: 'He made wonderful jokes, but he was such an unhappy man.'"

I sent an email to his and Jane's three children, asking if they thought that way about their father. "I would never sum my father up so simply!" Nanette protests. "I saw my father enjoy life as much as I saw him curse it. He was a very complex man who grew very unhappy and tired at the end of his life, but he wasn't always that way."

"He was a combat Vet with PTSD. He was unpredictable but not a particularly unhappy man," Mark says, rather briskly.

Edith said this to me earlier: "He wasn't bitter. He wasn't cynical. He was heartbroken by how humans treated each other. Maybe he had PTSD from just being alive. He saw too much. And he felt too much."

And as he neared his own death, he still made cracks. "The last thing I ever wanted was to be alive when the three most powerful people on the whole planet would be named Bush, Dick and Colon," he writes in *A Man Without a Country*, his last book published during his lifetime.

Still, it can be painful to read some of Vonnegut's last words. He was especially embittered by the US wars in Afghanistan and Iraq. "I've said everything I want to say, and I'm embarrassed to have lived this long," he told an interviewer in 2006. "I so envy Joseph Heller and George Plimpton and all these friends of mine who are pushing up daisies. They don't have to hear the news."

To reduce his life to his end of days would not only be very anti-Tralfamadorian but also an insult to the larger crusade that propelled Vonnegut throughout his writing career: to stand up for basic human dignity. He was taking on quite a load when he wrote *Slaughterhouse-Five*. He wanted to take on everything that ails us, not just war trauma. At the beginning of the book, after mentioning the inevitability of war, he widens the playing field: "And, even if wars didn't keep coming like glaciers, there would still be plain old death."

One of the great paradoxes Vonnegut confronted every time he sat at his typewriter is the same conundrum that faces us all: maintaining our integrity and a sense of humor despite knowing that we and everyone we know will one day die. In *Slaughterhouse-Five*, Vonnegut, as the author, speaks for all of us on the planet when he says, "I suppose they will all want dignity."

BEFORE VONNEGUT DIED on April 11, 2007, he wrote his final speech that was to be given at Clowes Hall at Butler University in Indianapolis as part of the city's "Year of Vonnegut" celebration on April 27. After he passed, his son, Mark, went to Indianapolis to read it.

The speech is filled with Vonnegut's satirical, wry humor: cracks about semicolons, himself, religion, and the *Mona Lisa*. And he hangs the talk on his pursuit of something that all Americans can agree upon. He is appalled at how our country has become "so tragically and ferociously divided." It's classic Vonnegut: He raises us higher by bringing us closer at the same time that he parodies our efforts and our differences.

What he addresses assails us even more today: global warming, the disparity of wealth, the dignity of Black people in the face of centuries of injustice, and the catastrophic consequences of misapplied technology. (It seems like the only major strains he misses are the potential for a deadly global pandemic, immigration issues, and the #MeToo movement—the latter, giving women their due, being Vonnegut's consistent weak spot.)

The striking relevance of the speech more than a decade later isn't surprising. Vonnegut understood the threads that make up our country. He studied them. His children remember him intently reading up on all of the terrible ways that humans treated each other. He had a penetrating insight into America's history of trauma. In the same way that he could anticipate PTSD, he knew the direction our nation was going.

Slaughterhouse-Five belongs to an estimable literary tradition. Most of our best books are about struggling to overcome hardship (*The Scarlet Letter, The Color Purple*), wrestle with the past (*The Great Gatsby, Native Son*), and defeat injustice (*Uncle Tom's Cabin, To Kill a Mockingbird*). Or, as Vonnegut would have it: "Do you realize that all great literature," he wrote, "are all about what a bummer it is to be a human being?" And coping with trauma through storytelling has marked how every generation has endured national crises such as the Civil War, the Great Depression, World War II, and the Vietnam War—all of which were painful experiences that were measured and assimilated through novels (*The Red Badge of Courage, The Grapes of Wrath, The*

Naked and the Dead, and so on). Our country has always moved forward, but not without the healing of powerful narratives.

That is one of the roles of the artist, and it's a particularly civic-minded one that Vonnegut believed in. He was more of a patriot than a revolutionary. "The American experience has been an unhappy experience, generally, and part of it . . . is living without a culture," he once said. "All my books are my effort to answer that question and to make myself like life better than I do."

In the year that *Slaughterhouse-Five* was published, Vonnegut gave a speech in which he mawkishly contemplated the role of the artist in this "vale of tears." He came up with a "canary-in-the-coal-mine theory of the arts." He said, "This theory argues that artists are useful to society because they are so sensitive." He joked that the "most useful thing" he could have done was to keel over before his speech in order to warn his audience of the state they were in.

Vonnegut lived the life of a canary longer than he would have liked, and it wore him down.

"My country is in ruins," he said in one of his last interviews when President George W. Bush was presiding over the wars in Iraq and Afghanistan. "There should have been hope. This should have been a great country. But we are despised all over the world now."

But still he didn't stop. He kept the zingers coming. He closed his 2007 Clowes Hall speech with one last heartfelt, prescient smirk: "And how should we behave during this Apocalypse? We should be unusually kind to one another, certainly. But we should also stop being so serious. Jokes help a lot. And get a dog, if you don't already have one."

The advice is so poignant. And apt. If he only knew the state we'd be in. But maybe he *did* know. And then he ended with "I myself just got a dog, and it's a new crossbreed. It's half French poodle and half Chinese shih tzu. It's a shit-poo. And I thank you for your attention, and I'm out of here."

You get it? His last public words were about his damn dog, the one that got him killed in the end. Talk about *Vonnegutian*. What a snort.

TEMPTING THOUGH IT MAY BE, I'd rather not leave you wrapped in that wet blanket. I'd prefer to end with something that Vonnegut wrote for the twenty-fifth anniversary edition of *Slaughterhouse-Five*, something that I wish all veterans of trauma and, really, all of us could absorb. It, too, honors his canine and Tralfamadorian friends and suggests Vonnegut may have come to terms with his past after all: "The British mathematician Stephen Hawking, in his 1988 bestseller, *A Brief History of Time*, found it tantalizing that we could not remember the future," he wrote. "But remembering the future is child's play for me now. I know what will become of my helpless, trusting babies because they are grown-ups now. I know how my closest friends will end up because so many of them are retired or dead now. . . . To Stephen Hawking and all others younger than myself I say: 'Be patient. Your future will come to you and lie down at your feet like a dog who knows and likes you no matter what you are.'"

Vonnegut may not have been Mr. Happy at the end of his life, or even over most of his existence on this planet. But these words indicate he had a profound understanding of acceptance. It would suggest he had made peace with those wolves at the door, including his memories of Dresden. At least, that is, on the page. And that's what he's left us.

If you haven't done so recently, I'd recommend reading or rereading *Slaughterhouse-Five*. It really holds up. I think of what Fred Greybar, the Vietnam vet who cried on the toilet, said to me. It tells you something different when you read it at different stages in your life. It's as if it time travels to meet you where you are.

Thank you for your attention. I, too, am out of here.

Vonnegut in 2006 in Barnstable, Cape Cod, photographed by Buck Squibb, one of his grandchildren. Courtesy of Buck Squibb.

AUTHOR'S NOTE

ALL THIS, TOO, HAPPENED:

In 1993, my first "job" out of college was a $75 per week internship at *The Nation* magazine. The interns were corralled into a windowless room with moldy carpeting and our so-called desks were one long shelf that ran along three walls. But it was a start, and I was thrilled to be working as the fact-checker and editorial assistant for writer Andy Kopkind.

One afternoon, the magazine's saucy octogenarian receptionist patched a call to the one telephone in the intern room and I picked it up. A gruff voice said, "Hello. This is Kurt Vonnegut. I'd like to ask you to do a job for me." There was a slight pause. "I'll pay you," he added.

Looking back, I'm surprised I wasn't more surprised. But I think I was too young to appreciate what I didn't know. My memory of the details of Vonnegut's assignment is hazy but what I recall is that he was amiable and he wanted me to look up the Khmer, or Cambodian, word for morning sun. He said he wanted to use that word for the name of one of his characters. He told me he'd pay me $50.

Yes, this was before the internet as we know it today. I looked up the word and called Vonnegut back. He was satisfied with my answer. He mailed me the check. What I most vividly remember of the whole encounter is the dilemma I then faced: Should I keep the check signed in unmistakable ink by the famous author, or should I cash it so that I could have the fifty bucks?

I figured it was too much money to turn down. At least I made a copy of the check before I cashed it. But I lost the copy.

Again, I'll say it: How *Vonnegutian*. Here's the trick about saying something is Vonnegutian: It is anything that strikes one as distinctly human, especially if it's steeped in irony and the absurd foibles of the human mind as it struggles against the advances of time and adversity. This applies to the most banal, dire, or perplexing of human challenges, be they death, bad luck, injustice, war, artistic expression, or contemplating one's own asshole. Vonnegut tackled them all, and he made them his own. And then he gave them back to us in stories or jokes or some other perceptive writing.

Nearly three decades after talking to him, Vonnegut reentered my life thanks to Jamison Stoltz, my editor at Abrams. This is the third in a series of "books on books" that Jamison is editing and Abrams is publishing. The first was *On Nineteen Eighty-Four* and the second, published earlier this year, was *In Search of The Color Purple.* I look forward to the next one.

Working on this book partly through the COVID-19 pandemic has been a ballast and a blast for me. Vonnegut was deeply concerned with what ails Americans. He tried to unpack the little traumas of everyday life as well as the big ones wrought by global events like the World Wars and the development of the atomic bomb. His writing grounded me throughout 2020.

There are so many of his insights that kept me going. I particularly liked what he said about *Hamlet*: "Shakespeare tells us we don't know enough about life to know what the good news and the bad news is." It felt germane partly because the last time I sat in a packed audience in 2020 I happened to see a production of *Hamlet* the night that New York governor Andrew Cuomo first declared a state of emergency. Here's another appropriate one from Vonnegut: "Keep your hat on. We may wind up miles from here."

Vonnegut was so clever and his communication of subtle, complex, hard truths made them so relatable. . . . And funny. It boggles my mind.

I spoke with many people about what it would have been like to have Vonnegut alive during the Trump presidency as well as during COVID. "That would have driven him up the wall," his friend Dan Wakefield said of our twice-impeached president. "It has been beyond satire."

So, my first thanks is to Mr. Vonnegut. My second is to Jamison. And my third is to my sources, especially Matthew Mellina and Lance Miccio and the others who opened themselves up to me about their personal experiences with trauma.

Vonnegut's three oldest children, Mark, Edith, and Nanette, were also foundational to my ability to write this book. Visiting both Edith and Nanette in their respective homes in Massachusetts allowed me to feel like I could breathe the air that Kurt once inhaled. The sisters are both accomplished painters with glimmers of their father's earthbound magic, as well as his charm and eccentricity, and they enriched me with their warm hospitality and insight. Speaking of inhaling, Edith allowing me to sit in Vonnegut's writing room (where he wrote *Slaughterhouse-Five*!) and smoke his actual Pall Malls—he bought a case before he died—is something I'll never forget.

Also keeping the Vonnegut legacy alive is the Kurt Vonnegut Museum and Library, which is led by its CEO and founder, Julia Whitehead, a dedicated veteran with a vision. Visit it if you can. And the Lilly Library, which Kurt entrusted with the preservation of his work and papers, was a reliable resource and is a worthy host of his oeuvre. I am grateful for its help. And then Vonnegut's other primary stewards are the Vonnegut scholars, the academics and writers who have made his life work part of their own: Christina Jarvis, Jerome Klinkowitz, and Marc Leeds have been generous with their time and knowledge. I never spoke with Peter Reed and William Rodney Allen, but their writing, along with that of Donald Fiene, helped me greatly. And, as I hope I have made clear throughout, Charles Shields's detailed biography was invaluable to me.

Of course, the undercard on this project has always been Tim O'Brien. He may be a different kind of writer than Vonnegut, but he is as worthy of our appreciation and close attention. He also happens to be the greatest living embodiment of the great American war writer. Not that he should be boxed into being one kind of writer, but that's the role he served for my book, so that's how I mostly see him. I placed great value on what he said to me. And I was moved by how gracious, congenial, and disarmingly reflective he was in conversation. Speaking with him was a highlight of this project. And then to toggle between him and his protégé, Matt Gallagher, a veteran and writer still coming into his own, gave my own process a strong sense of relevance. Matt was also a giving source. These guys, along with Mellina, Miccio, and Fred Greybar, have given me a deeper appreciation for a unique, special breed of human being, the book-loving, thoughtful veteran.

This book is about how an author was able to write about the trauma of war. And what we can carry from that. I looked at it from a psychological and literary perspective, so thank goodness I could lean on psychiatrists, such as Robert Jay Lifton, Jonathan Shay, and Harold Kudler, who understand the role literature can play in navigating the pain of war.

In addition to my many sources, I give much thanks to my friends and family—loving props to my Brooklyn pod, Sandee, Natalie, and Maxine—who have supported me throughout the writing of this book. And a special nod to Neil Pergament, my first reader and good friend, who is as adept at discussing Vonnegut as he is Robert Caro, Bruce Springsteen, and the early work of Ben Affleck. And a huzzah to Marly Rusoff, my agent, for her excellent agenting.

There's a Swahili saying that film director George Miller quoted in an interview I read while working on *The Writer's Crusade*: "The story has been told. If it was bad, it was my fault, because I am the storyteller. But if it was good, it belongs to everybody."

I like that. But it's a little grandiose for my little book. I think I should take responsibility for the former, but let's agree that the latter just applies to *Slaughterhouse-Five*. My book is just the window through which I hope we can better see Vonnegut's masterpiece for what it is: something that belongs to all of us, and is still well worth reading today.

A NON-TRALFAMADORIAN
TIMELINE OF VONNEGUT'S LIFE

November 11, 1922: Kurt Vonnegut Jr. is born in Indianapolis, Indiana, the son of Kurt Sr. and Edith Vonnegut.

September 1940: Vonnegut enrolls at Cornell University but before flunking out, he enlists in the army in January 1943.

May 14, 1944: Edith Vonnegut dies.

December 19, 1945: Vonnegut is captured by the Germans during the Battle of the Bulge.

February 13–14, 1945: The bombing of Dresden.

May 29, 1945: Vonnegut writes a letter to his family announcing he is alive and recuperating at Camp Lucky Strike repatriation camp in Le Havre and soon to be on his way back to the States.

September 1, 1945: Vonnegut and Jane Cox get married.

December 1945: Mr. and Mrs. Vonnegut move to Chicago to study at the University of Chicago.

May 11, 1947: Mark Vonnegut is born.

September 1947: Vonnegut gets a job in the public relations department at GE in Schenectady, New York.

December 29, 1949: Kurt and Jane's second child, Edith, is born in Schenectady, New York.

February 11, 1950: Vonnegut's first short story, "The Barnhouse Effect," is published in *Collier's* magazine.

Fall, 1951: Vonnegut family moves to Cape Cod, Massachusetts.

1952: *Player Piano* is published.

October 4, 1954: Kurt and Jane's third child, Nanette, is born in Cape Cod.

February 1955: Vonnegut family moves to a sprawling house in West Barnstable, Cape Cod.

September 1958: Kurt's sister, Alice, dies less than two days after his brother-in-law, Jim Adams, dies in a train crash. Vonnegut family adopts three Adams boys; Tiger, Steve, and Jim Jr.

1959: *Sirens of Titan* is published.

1961: *Mother Night* is published.

1963: *Cat's Cradle* is published.

1964: Vonnegut visits friend Bernard V. O'Hare to discuss their experiences in Dresden and Mary O'Hare confronts Vonnegut. "You were just babies in the war," she says. (Vonnegut suggests this happened in 1965 but it is more likely that it occurred in 1964.)

1965: *God Bless You, Mr. Rosewater* is published.

September 1965: Vonnegut begins two-year teaching gig at Iowa Writers' Workshop.

October 1967: Vonnegut visits Dresden with O'Hare on a Guggenheim Fellowship grant.

June 1968: Vonnegut mails the final draft of *Slaughterhouse-Five* to his publisher.

March 1969: *Slaughterhouse-Five* is published.

1971: Vonnegut moves from Barnstable to live permanently in New York City.

1971: University of Chicago belatedly accepts *Cat's Cradle* as his thesis, earning him his master's degree.

March 1972: *Slaughterhouse-Five*, the movie, is released in theaters, garnering generally positive reviews but tepid box office.

1973: *Breakfast of Champions* is published.

February 13, 1976: Fictional character Billy Pilgrim is assassinated; real-life author Vonnegut receives condolence letters in the mail.

1976: *Slapstick* is published.

1979: Vonnegut and Jill Krementz are married.

1979: *Jailbird* is published.

1982: *Deadeye Dick* is published.

December 1982: Vonnegut and Krementz adopt their daughter, Lily.

1984: Vonnegut attempts suicide, fails.

1985: *Galápagos* is published.

December 19, 1986: Jane passes away.

1987: *Bluebeard* is published.

1990: *Hocus Pocus* is published.

1991: When asked in *Playboy* what he is working on, Vonnegut says, "A divorce. Which is a full-time job." But despite marital strains, he and Krementz remain together.

1997: *Timequake* is published.

1998: Vonnegut returns to Dresden and visits the slaughterhouse where he was imprisoned during World War II.

1998: Vonnegut begins a radio series of interviews with deceased people, *Reports on the Afterlife*, for WNYC. Interviewees include Sir Isaac Newton, Eugene Debs, and Adolf Hitler.

2000: After an accidental fire in his New York City home, Vonnegut engages in an unsuccessful stint teaching creative writing at Smith, a women's college in Northampton, Massachusetts. His daughter, Nanette, and three adopted nephews, live nearby.

2005: *A Man Without a Country*, a book of Vonnegut's more recent essays in which he makes cracks, decries the George W. Bush presidency, and calls for basic human decency, is published.

April 11, 2007: Vonnegut dies.

NOTES

What follows is information about sourcing and other notes, in case you are interested. If you have questions or comments or otherwise want to share, drop me a line at www.tomroston.com/contact.

CHAPTER ONE

Regarding revenge and most things epistemological, my go-to is Binghamton University associate professor of philosophy and lifelong friend Melissa Zinkin. Melissa also directed me to the *Stanford Encyclopedia of Philosophy.*

All quotes from Vonnegut's early drafts at the Lilly Library are courtesy of Kurt Vonnegut LLC and the Wylie Agency LLC and the Lilly Library, Indiana University, Bloomington, Indiana.

As of the printing of this book, Brian Welke's book hadn't yet been published, but I hope it soon will be and I imagine an internet search will get you to it.

Much thanks to Vicki Jones Cole for the information she shared and her permission to use this dedication page of the copy of *Slaughterhouse-Five* that belonged to her father, Tom Jones.

"The war had been a great adventure to me, which I wouldn't have missed for anything" comes from *Fates Worse Than Death* (p. 156).

Paul Fussell's quote comes from "My War," *Harper's* magazine, January 1982.

CHAPTER TWO

William Deresiewicz, "'I Was There': On Kurt Vonnegut," *The Nation* magazine, June 4, 2012.

Arnold Edelstein's essay, "Billy's Time Travel Is Not Science Fictional but Psychological," appears in *War in Kurt Vonnegut's* Slaughterhouse-Five.

Salman Rushdie, "What Kurt Vonnegut's 'Slaughterhouse-Five' Tells Us Now," *New Yorker* online, June 13, 2019.

Malcolm Jack, "From Dresden on the 50th Anniversary of 'Slaughterhouse-Five,'" *New York Times*, March 21, 2019.

The estimate of 125,000 copies of *Slaughterhouse-Five* being sold in 2019 comes from NPDBookscan.

Connecting with Jerome Klinkowitz was a real boon for the project. Not only has he written a ton on Vonnegut, but he was also readily available to me for insights into *Slaughterhouse-Five* and the rest of Vonnegut's career. And he, like Dan Wakefield, made me feel like I was in Kurt's presence. Klinkowitz doesn't use email, so his frequent typewritten notes and instructions were welcome messages seemingly from a bygone, or I should say "unstuck," time. He also sent me a box of books that I am very grateful for.

Alex Horton wrote a great piece, "Reading 'Slaughterhouse-Five' in Baghdad: What Vonnegut Taught Me About What Comes After War," for the *Washington Post*, April 13, 2019.

Suicide rates and statistics regarding PTSD come mostly from the 2020 National Veteran Suicide Prevention Annual Report, US Department of Veterans Affairs, the National Institute of

Mental Health website, and the *New York Times*. The 2020 report indicates that the veteran suicide rate is 27.5 per 100,000 and the National Institute of Mental Health records a rate of 14.2 suicides per 100,000 Americans.

CHAPTER THREE

"People deprived of the dignified postures by gravity" comes from *Timequake* (p. 117) and I hope you caught that "Bloompity, bloomp, bloomp" also comes from *Timequake*. It's what Vonnegut said of the guy from the gas company who fell down the basement stairs.

Restoring the family fortune comes from Mark Vonnegut's *Just Like Someone Without Mental Illness* (p. 15).

In addition to John Rauch's "An Account of the Ancestry of Kurt Vonnegut, Jr., by an Ancient Friend of His Family," I used *And So It Goes* by Charles Shields and published interviews with Vonnegut, especially 1973's *Playboy*, for a great deal of the Vonnegut family history. And special thanks to Indianapolis's own local historian, William Selm, who was a knowledgeable and homespun resource who gave me insights into the Vonnegut-Indianapolis connection.

Kurt's entry into the army and early years primarily comes from letters that he wrote, most of which were reprinted in Wakefield's *Kurt Vonnegut: Letters*. I also used *The Brothers Vonnegut* by Ginger Strand.

Kurt's early years with Jane are probably best illustrated in *Love, Kurt: The Vonnegut Love Letters, 1941–1945*, edited by Edith Vonnegut. That book came out at the end of 2020 as I was finishing mine, so instead I used interviews with Nanette and Edith, Kurt's other letters, *And So It Goes*, and Strand's "How

Jane Vonnegut Made Kurt Vonnegut a Writer," published in the *New Yorker* online on December 3, 2015. The mental health issues come up in *Just Like Someone Without Mental Illness* and *Fates Worse than Death* (p. 155).

My sources for the death of Vonnegut's mother are primarily Vonnegut's writing in *Palm Sunday* and *Fates Worse than Death*, and *And So It Goes*. It's worth noting that Vonnegut's children aren't convinced that their grandmother meant to kill herself and believe that it may have been an accidental overdose. But I am going by Kurt's assessment.

Vonnegut said, "She got depressed over what was going on in Germany," in "The Long Happy Life of Kurt Vonnegut," *Haaretz*, October 12, 2002.

Vonnegut's experience in the war comes from his recollections in his many interviews and nonfiction writing, *And So It Goes*, Ervin Szpek's *Shadows of Slaughterhouse Five*, and "From the 'Bulge' to Dresden: A Soldier's Odyssey" by veterans H. Lew Wallace and William R. Burns, published in the 1986 publication of "Perspectives in History" in the *Journal of the Alpha Beta Phi Chapter of Phi Alpha Theta*. I also used Szpek's "My Service Memoirs" on www.indianamilitary.org, under the auspices of the US Army and AmVets of Indiana. The same site also reprinted an interview of Slaughterhouse Five POW Gifford Doxsee by Daniel Sturm that ran in the *Athens News* on May 3, 2007, which was enlightening. Vonnegut's conversation with Joseph Heller on the fiftieth anniversary of V-E Day at the University of New Orleans was also good; it's on YouTube. And Brian Welke's talk at the Kurt Vonnegut Museum and Library on November 9, 2019, filled in the gaps.

In 2004, the mayor of Dresden commissioned a report on the actual number of casualties during 1945's Dresden bombing. The highly reputable commission of German historians used a variety of sources including new archival material that established that the number was closer to 25,000 civilians killed. For more information on the report, "Dresden Commission of Historians for the Ascertainment of the Number of Victims of the Air Raids on the City of Dresden on 13/14 February 1945," see "Panel Rethinks Death Toll from Dresden Raids" in the *Guardian* (October 2, 2008) and "How Many Died in the Bombing of Dresden?," *Der Spiegel* (February 10, 2008).

Whether or not Dresden was a legitimate target is explored in Frederick Taylor's *Dresden: Tuesday, February 13, 1945*. George Packer also wrote a good piece on the subject called "Embers" in the January 25, 2010, issue of the *New Yorker*.

CHAPTER FOUR

As in chapter three, Jane and Kurt's early years come from Vonnegut's letters in *Kurt Vonnegut: Letters*, "How Jane Vonnegut Made Kurt Vonnegut a Writer" by Strand, the *New Yorker*, December 3, 2015, interviews with Vonnegut children, and *And So It Goes*. For Vonnegut's early career as a writer, *Kurt Vonnegut: Letters* was instrumental. I also used the Klinkowitz and Wakefield-edited *Kurt Vonnegut: Complete Stories*, Gregory Sumner's *Unstuck in Time: A Journey through Kurt Vonnegut's Life and Novels*, Strand's *The Brothers Vonnegut*, Klinkowitz's *Kurt Vonnegut's America*, and *And So It Goes*.

Nanette told Charles Shields the story of her father sobbing after almost driving off a bridge the day she was born.

Vonnegut called his former students "seriously fucked-up rich kids" in *Timequake* (p. 15).

The death of Kurt's sister, Alice, and the adoption of her children comes from *Kurt Vonnegut: Letters*, clips, *And So It Goes*, and Jane's *Angels Without Wings*.

Life in Barnstable comes from *And So It Goes*, *Kurt Vonnegut: Letters* and interviews with Edith and Nanette Vonnegut.

The H. G. Wells anecdote is in *And So It Goes*.

See the bibliography for the lit crit books about Vonnegut's work for my tour through his novels; especially helpful was *Kurt Vonnegut's America* and my interviews with Jerry Klinkowitz and Christina Jarvis.

Vonnegut took his reviews to heart. He even wore them as a badge; he quoted the *New Yorker*'s "a series of narcissistic giggles" snipe in the preface to his collection *Welcome to the Monkey House*.

CHAPTER FIVE

I got much of the research for this chapter from my interviews with Professor Jarvis, Vonnegut's letters in *Kurt Vonnegut: Letters*, and the archives at the Lilly Library. I cannot thank Jarvis enough for showing me the Sam Stewart letter. It is her discovery and it is a crucial one that deepens our understanding that Vonnegut was further along in writing the book before he went to Iowa than he represented. Jarvis showed this to me in the pure spirit of shared knowledge and appreciation for Vonnegut's work.

"Everything that was reported by ace newsmen" was in Strand's *New Yorker* article.

The Tom Jones quote comes from Vicki Jones Cole.

The teleplays ("I'll Go to Sleep in Dresden," "A Dresden Goodnight," and "Slaughterhouse-Five") are in the archives at the Lilly

Library and the "the deeply disturbing truth" quote is courtesy of the Kurt Vonnegut LLC and the Wylie Agency LLC and the Lilly Library, Indiana University, Bloomington, Indiana.

Vonnegut muses about New Journalism in the preface to *Wampeters, Foma and Granfalloons.*

Vonnegut's America and *Vonnegut in Fact* were excellent sources for Vonnegut's writing during the early 1960s, including "Vonnegut" being, in an earlier version, the narrator's name in *Cat's Cradle.*

The Theodore Sturgeon anecdote comes from *And So It Goes.*

The *Treasure Island*–Caroline Kennedy anecdote comes from a Vonnegut letter in *Kurt Vonnegut: Letters* (p. 101).

Vonnegut's time in Iowa primarily comes from *Kurt Vonnegut: Letters, And So It Goes* (where I got the Suzanne McConnell anecdote), and *Love as Always, Kurt: Vonnegut as I Knew Him.*

In conversation, Klinkowitz helped underscore the significance of the *Mother Night* introduction for me.

Once again, I'll note that all of the forays into the discarded drafts are thanks to the Lilly Library and Kurt Vonnegut LLC, which graciously gave me permission to quote from them. I hope that one day someone will properly organize those records, especially dating the drafts, at the Lilly. Not that you asked, but I nominate Professor Jarvis.

CHAPTER SIX

"Largely a found object" comes from Vonnegut's July 1973 interview published in *Playboy*, probably the most revealing and instructive interview of his life.

There are a couple of videotaped versions of Vonnegut's "Fluctuations Between Good and Ill Fortune in Simple Tales" lecture that can be found on YouTube. Check them out. And enjoy the rough edges, especially his smoker's hacking laughter.

Roethke's poem "The Waking" is well worth reading in full.

CHAPTER SEVEN

Vonnegut's recollections of his war experiences have stood the test of time; his many printed statements haven't been challenged that I know of. Also, as noted in chapter three, I found significant corroboration of Vonnegut's incredible war experiences from his fellow Slaughterhouse Five POWs as seen in Ervin Szpek's *Shadows of Slaughterhouse Five* and from veterans H. Lew Wallace, William R. Burns, and Gifford Doxsee. And, likewise, Brian Welke's research helped support Vonnegut's "war parts."

Independent accounts of Michael Palaia and Joe Crone come from Szpek's *Shadows of Slaughterhouse Five* and the sources mentioned in the previous note. Also, Vonnegut spoke of Crone in the *Rochester Democrat and Chronicle* on May 3, 1995. *And So It Goes* is an additional source. My conversations with Klinkowitz further supported my understanding of both Michael Palaia and Joe Crone.

Vonnegut's multiple attempts at constructing the Michael Palaia and Edward "Joe" Crone characters are at the Lilly Library, Indiana University, Bloomington, Indiana, and the quotes are courtesy of the Lilly Library and Vonnegut LLC.

Vonnegut made the Hitler-Stalin crack at what sounds like a wild and contentious seminar entitled "The Conscience of the Writer." The quote was reported in *Publishers Weekly*, March 22, 1971, and reprinted in *Conversations with Kurt Vonnegut*.

"I did what I did without knowing what I was doing" is from the *Haaretz* interview.

CHAPTER EIGHT

Benedict Kimmelman's article, "The Example of Private Slovik," in the September/October 1987 issue of *American Heritage* was a great resource.

Theodore Roosevelt is reputedly the source of the quote, "I could carve a better man out of a banana," but the twenty-sixth president actually said, "I could carve out of a banana a judge with more backbone than that," referring to Supreme Court Justice Oliver Wendell Holmes, whom he perceived as having betrayed him.

I used a number of papers, articles, and books for background on the history of war trauma, including, "When Nostalgia Was a Disease" (2013, *The Atlantic*), *Nostalgia and Recollection in Victorian Culture* (1998, Palgrave Macmillan), *Nostalgia: A "Forgotten" Psychological Disorder* (2009, *Psychological Medicine*), "'Railway spine'? 'Soldier's heart'? Try 'PTSD,'" (2013, *Philadelphia Inquirer*), "DaCosta's Syndrome" (2001, *Lancet*), "The Shock of War" (2010, *Smithsonian* magazine), *A War of Nerves* (2001, Harvard University Press), "From Shell Shock and War Neurosis to Posttraumatic Disorder" (2001, *Dialogues in Clinical Neuroscience*), *Mental Hygiene* (1919, National Association for Mental Health publication), *Neuropsychiatry* (1929, the Medical Department of the United States Army in the World War report for the US Surgeon General's Office), *The History and Influence of the American Psychiatric Association* (1987, American Psychiatric Association Publishing), "War &

Military Mental Health: The US Psychiatric Response in the 20th Century" (2007, *American Journal of Public Health*), *War Neuroses* (1945, Blakiston), "Current Trends in Military Neuropsychiatry" (1944, *American Journal of Psychiatry*), *Controversial Issues in Health Care Policy* (1993, Sage Publications), "Posttraumatic Stress Disorder and the Nature of Trauma" (2000, *Dialogues in Clinical Neuroscience*), "Psychiatric Experiences in the War, 1941–1946 (1947, *American Journal of Psychiatry*), "Examining Post-Traumatic Stress Disorder and the Plight of Vietnam Veterans" (2015, the University of Iowa *Undergraduate History Journal*), *War and Redemption: Treatment and Recovery in Combat-Related Posttraumatic Stress Disorder* (2004, Ashgate Publishing), "Post-Traumatic Stress Disorder in the Military Veteran" (1994, Psychiatric Clinics of North America publication), "Prevalence of PTSD Symptoms in Combat Veterans Seeking Medical Treatment" (1990, *Journal of Traumatic Stress*), "War Psychiatry" (1995, Office of the Surgeon General of the United States of America), "Psychiatry and the 'Lessons of Vietnam': What Were They, and Are They Still Relevant?" (2004, *War & Society*), "US Army Psychiatry in the Vietnam War" (2015, Borden Institute/US Department of Defense), "Disparate Prevalence Estimates of PTSD Among Service Members Who Served in Iraq and Afghanistan: Possible Explanations" (2010, *Journal of Traumatic Stress*), "Gulf War Illness and the Health of Gulf War Veterans: Research Update and Recommendations, 2009–2013" (2014, report by Research Advisory Committee on Gulf War Veterans' Illnesses, US Department of Veterans Affairs), and "Improvised Explosive Devices (IEDs) in Iraq and Afghanistan: Effects and Countermeasures" (2006, Congressional Research Service).

Chaim F. Shatan's "Post-Vietnam Syndrome" article appeared in the May 6, 1972, issue of the *New York Times*. I also used Patrick Hagopian's *The Vietnam War in American Memory* (University of Massachusetts Press) for background on Shatan and Lifton. My understanding of PTSD relied on interviews with Dr. Harold Kudler, Dr. Robert Jay Lifton, Dr. Jonathan Shay, and David Morris's *The Evil Hours*. I also leaned heavily on the US Department of Veterans Affairs website and its published materials as well as the following; the *New York Times* and the websites of the National Alliance of Mental Illness and American Psychiatric Association and the following publications: "Treatment for Posttraumatic Stress Disorder in Military and Veteran Populations" (2012, Committee on the Assessment of Ongoing Effects in the Treatment of Posttraumatic Stress Disorder, Institute of Medicine, the National Academies Press), "Posttraumatic Stress Disorder Post Iraq and Afghanistan: Prevalence Among Military Subgroups" (2014, *Canadian Journal of Psychiatry*), "Invisible Wounds of War Project" (2008, RAND Corporation), "Acknowledging the Psychiatric Cost of War" (2004, *New England Journal of Medicine*), "Combat and Operational Stress Control" (2016, US Marine Corps Publication), "Battlemind Training: Building Soldier Resiliency" (2006, Walter Reed Army Institute of Research Department of Military Psychiatry), and "How PTSD Became a Problem Far Beyond the Battlefield" (2015, *Vanity Fair*).

Lifton's "Survivor as Creator" appeared in the January/February 1973 issue of the *American Poetry Review*.

That there could be more than 500,000 mentally wounded American veterans from the engagements in Afghanistan and Iraq comes from several studies and articles mentioned above, but primarily from "Invisible Wounds of War Project" (2008, RAND Corporation).

CHAPTER NINE

The VA compensation rates can be found on its website.

The *American Journal of Public Health* article referred to here, "US Department of Veterans Affairs Disability Policies for Posttraumatic Stress Disorder: Administrative Trends and Implications for Treatment, Rehabilitation, and Research," was originally published in December 2007.

For malingering, I used papers published in the *Journal of the American Academy of Psychiatry and the Law* ("A Systematic Approach to the Detection of False PTSD," June 2019) and *Clinical Psychology Review* ("Apparent Symptom Overreporting in Combat Veterans Evaluated for PTSD," October 2000), among other reports.

The Boston study, "Klotho, PTSD, and Advanced Epigenetic Age in Cortical Tissue," ran in *Neuropsychopharmacology*, 2020.

Again, I relied mostly on the VA's published reports on PTSD for statistics and definitions.

Matt Gallagher has written a lot of good pieces, but my favorite, which I reference in this chapter, is "Pilgrim's Progress," *New York Times*, January 19, 2011.

I relied on Matthew Mellina for his story. I sought to corroborate information when I put into print the names of other people whom we discussed, such as Justin Jarrett and Ian Weikel. I am trusting that the truth of Mellina's story, if not exact details, is accurate. He and I discussed how different memories and perspectives could present a *Rashomon*-like representation of the events he described. I hope you and I can agree to view his story in that light.

The VA's PTSD treatments are well detailed on its website.

Mellina's *New York Times* pieces are "For a Veteran, Finding Reasons to Move Forward," (December 5, 2011) and "Don't Ask" (March 18, 2013). Check 'em out!

CHAPTER TEN

The VA's National Center for PTSD brochure, *Understanding PTSD and PTSD Treatment,* can be found on the publications page at www.ptsd.va.gov.

Vonnegut's interview "Kurt Vonnegut on Dresden," with Lee Roloff, can be found in *Kurt Vonnegut's Slaughterhouse-Five,* edited by Harold Bloom.

CHAPTER ELEVEN

As with Mellina, I relied on Lance Miccio for his story. I corroborated what I could when it came to the USS *Guam* and people whose names appear here in print. Miccio is a great storyteller, but that doesn't necessarily mean everything he told me happened just so. Still, he's a truth-teller.

The "I blew my cork" quote comes from David Standish's 1973 talk with Vonnegut that appears in *Playboy.* I don't know if Standish deserves the credit or if Vonnegut was feeling particularly open when they spoke, but this interview truly is a treasure.

Vonnegut often spoke of his depression, including in letters that are in *Vonnegut: The Letters* and in various interviews, such as the one in *Haaretz.* "Profoundly depressed" specifically comes from what he told *Sanity Plea* author Lawrence Broer.

What I refer to as an "unusually candid interview from 1996" is "Kurt Vonnegut on Dresden" with Lee Roloff, reprinted in *Kurt Vonnegut's Slaughterhouse-Five.*

The Anthony Burgess quotes come from a long interview he did with *Playboy* in its September 1974 issue.

CHAPTER TWELVE

Salman Rushdie, "What Kurt Vonnegut's 'Slaughterhouse-Five' Tells Us Now," *New Yorker* online, June 13, 2019.

"I didn't have to write at all anymore" comes from the July 1973 *Playboy* interview, which can be found in *Conversations with Kurt Vonnegut*, edited by William Rodney Allen.

As I will keep saying, I am indebted to Shields for his thorough research, which I again relied upon for this chapter. And the January 24, 1971, *New York Times Magazine* article, "The Masks of Kurt Vonnegut, Jr.," written by Richard Todd, is a good snapshot of Vonnegut's life at that time.

The letters to Nanette appear in *Kurt Vonnegut: Letters*.

My characterization of Vonnegut's marriage with Krementz comes from *And So It Goes* and my interviews.

Thanks to Professor Christina Jarvis for her insights into *Bluebeard*.

The quoted letters to Loree Rackstraw appear in her book, *Love as Always, Kurt: Vonnegut as I Knew Him*.

As cited in an earlier note, the story of Crone as the source of Billy Pilgrim was first published in the *Rochester Democrat and Chronicle* on May 3, 1995. The story behind Vonnegut's Rochester visit is well-reported by local historian and teacher David Kramer in his March 18, 2019, post on www.talkerof thetown.com.

CHAPTER THIRTEEN

Matthew Thomas wrote a book review roundup in December 2014, "A Year in Reading," for the website www.themillions.com.

Vonnegut refers to the "supreme irony" in a letter in *Kurt Vonnegut: The Letters* (p. 43).

Audie Murphy's quote "They took Army dogs and rehabilitated them for civilian life" was part of a story that ran on the AP on November 21, 1960; "I don't think they ever do" comes from Murphy's *New York Times* obituary on June 1, 1971.

Malcolm Gladwell's "Getting Over It" ran in the November 8, 2004, issue of the *New Yorker*. Read it in its entirety and see what you think.

Principal author Bruce Rind's 1998 *Psychological Bulletin* paper, "A Meta-Analytic Examination of Assumed Properties of Child Sexual Abuse Using College Samples," has been the subject of fierce debate, which Gladwell casts as a contest over political correctness, but the paper has also been criticized for methodology.

Roy Scranton's "War and the City: March Song" was published on the *New York Times* website on September 3, 2010.

Vonnegut says, "I was hoping to build a country and add to its literature," in *US Airways* magazine, one of his last interviews, which was published posthumously in June 2007. It was reprinted in *Kurt Vonnegut: The Last Interview.*

"They didn't want to talk about it" is from the 1973 *Playboy* interview.

CHAPTER FOURTEEN

The 1954 letter to Knox Burger is in *Kurt Vonnegut: Letters*.

Shields called Vonnegut a "disenchanted, angry adolescent" in a speech he posted on his website, www.charlesjshields.net.

"He made wonderful jokes, but he was such an unhappy man" is from the *Playboy* interview.

Vonnegut said, "I'm embarrassed to have lived this long," to J. C. Gabel in an interview first published in *Stop Smiling* magazine in 2006; it was republished in *Kurt Vonnegut: The Last Interview.*

Vonnegut's Clowes Hall speech was reprinted in *Armageddon in Retrospect* (2009).

"What a bummer" is from *A Man Without a Country.*

"The American experience has been an unhappy experience" is from the *Playboy* interview.

"Canary-in-the-coal-mine theory of the arts" is in *Wampeters, Foma and Granfalloons.*

"My country is in ruins" is from the *US Airways* magazine interview.

Thanks to the Vonnegut Museum and Library's Chris Lafave for sending me Vonnegut's introduction to the twenty-fifth anniversary edition of *Slaughterhouse-Five*, in which Vonnegut wrote that "remembering the future is child's play for me now." I'm delighted that sublime science fiction writer Ted Chiang was also inspired by Vonnegut's quote. Chiang credits it for summing up the theme of his wonderful "Story of Your Life," which was turned into the film *Arrival.* It seems fitting to end with a beginning.

BIBLIOGRAPHY

VONNEGUT'S NONFICTION BOOKS AND
COLLECTIONS THAT I'D RECOMMEND:
Welcome to the Monkey House (1968)
Wampeters, Foma and Granfalloons (1974)
Palm Sunday (1981)
Fates Worse Than Death (1991)
A Man Without a Country (2005)
Armageddon in Retrospect (2008)
If This Isn't Nice, What Is?: Advice to the Young (2013)
Vonnegut by the Dozen (2013)
Kurt Vonnegut: Letters (2014)
Complete Stories: Kurt Vonnegut (2017)
Love, Kurt: The Vonnegut Love Letters, 1941–1945 (2020)

NONFICTION BOOKS ABOUT *SLAUGHTERHOUSE-
FIVE* OR KURT VONNEGUT:
And So It Goes (Henry Holt and Co., 2011), Charles Shields.
The Brothers Vonnegut (Farrar, Straus and Giroux, 2015), Ginger
   Strand.
Conversations with Kurt Vonnegut (University Press of Mississippi,
   1988), edited by William Rodney Allen.

Critical Essays on Kurt Vonnegut (G. K. Hall, 1990), edited by Robert Merrill.

Critical Insights: Slaughterhouse-Five (Salem Press, 2010), edited by Leonard Mustazza.

The Critical Response to Kurt Vonnegut (Greenwood Press, 1994), edited by Leonard Mustazza.

The Fabulators (Oxford University Press, 1967), Robert Scholes.

Kurt Vonnegut: A Critical Companion (Greenwood Press, 2002), Thomas F. Marvin.

Kurt Vonnegut: The Last Interview and Other Conversations (Melville House, 2011), edited by Tom McCartan.

Kurt Vonnegut's America (University of South Carolina Press, 2009), Jerome Klinkowitz.

Kurt Vonnegut's Slaughterhouse-Five (Chelsea House Publications, 2009), edited by Harold Bloom.

Love as Always, Kurt: Vonnegut as I Knew Him (Da Capo Press, 2009), Loree Rackstraw.

Sanity Plea: Schizophrenia in the Novels of Kurt Vonnegut (University of Alabama Press, 1994), Lawrence R. Broer.

Shadows of Slaughterhouse Five (iUniverse, 2008), Ervin Szpek Jr. and Frank Idzikowski.

Slaughterhouse-Five: Reforming the Novel and the World (Twayne Publishers, 1989), Jerome Klinkowitz.

Understanding Kurt Vonnegut (University of South Carolina Press, 2009), William Rodney Allen.

Unstuck in Time: A Journey Through Kurt Vonnegut's Life and Novels (Seven Stories Press, 2011), Gregory Sumner.

The Vonnegut Effect (University of South Carolina Press, 2004), Jerome Klinkowitz.

The Vonnegut Encyclopedia (Delacorte Press, 1994), Marc Leeds.

Vonnegut in Fact (University of South Carolina Press, 1998), Jerome Klinkowitz.

War in Kurt Vonnegut's Slaughterhouse-Five (Greenhaven Press, 2011), edited by Claudia Durst Johnson.

NONFICTION BOOKS ABOUT WAR AND/OR TRAUMA:

Achilles in Vietnam: Combat Trauma and the Undoing of Character (Scribner, 2010), Robert Shay.

The Body Keeps the Score: Brain, Mind, and Body in the Healing of Trauma (Penguin Books, 2015), Bessel van der Kolk.

The Evil Hours: A Biography of Posttraumatic Stress Disorder (Houghton Mifflin Harcourt, 2015), David Morris.

Kaboom: Embracing the Suck in a Savage Little War (Da Capo Press, 2010), Matt Gallagher.

Shook Over Hell: Post-Traumatic Stress, Vietnam, and the Civil War (Harvard University Press, 1999), Eric T. Dean Jr.

Trauma and Recovery (Basic Books, 1992), Judith Herman.

A War of Nerves (Harvard University Press, 2003), Ben Shephard.

What It Is Like to Go to War (Grove Atlantic, 2011), by Karl Marlantes.

WAR NOVELS AND STORY COLLECTIONS THAT CONTRIBUTED TO MY THINKING:

All Quiet on the Western Front, by Erich Maria Remarque

Billy Lynn's Long Halftime Walk, by Ben Fountain

Catch-22, by Joseph Heller

A Farewell to Arms, by Ernest Hemingway

Fire and Forget, edited by Roy Scranton and Matt Gallagher

For Whom the Bell Tolls, by Ernest Hemingway

Going After Cacciato, by Tim O'Brien

The Naked and the Dead, by Norman Mailer

The Red Badge of Courage, by Stephen Crane
Redeployment, by Phil Klay
The Things They Carried, by Tim O'Brien
The Yellow Birds, by Kevin Powers
Youngblood, by Matt Gallagher

OTHER IMPORTANT BOOKS:
Angels Without Wings, by Jane Vonnegut Yarmolinsky
Dad's Maybe Book, by Tim O'Brien
The Eden Express, by Mark Vonnegut
Just Like Someone Without Mental Illness Only More So, by Mark
   Vonnegut

INDEX

If you are looking for help for PTSD-related symptoms and you are a veteran—or if you know a veteran who needs help—visit https://www.ptsd.va.gov. If you are a veteran in crisis (or are worried about one), call 1-800-273-8255 and press "1" (or text 838255). And for everyone, there's also the Anxiety and Depression Association of America, which has a robust website (https://adaa.org) where you can connect with local mental health care providers. If you need help right now, you can also text HOME to 741741 to connect with a crisis counselor from the Crisis Text Line. I am not a professional in this field, so these are only suggestions.

Veterans looking for writing workshops should consider NYU's Words After War, which Matt Gallagher teaches; Warrior Writers, a Philadelphia-based nonprofit (www.warriorwriters.org); the United States Veterans' Artists Alliance Writing Program (www.usvaa.org); and the Writer's Guild Foundation's Veterans Writing Project (www.wgfoundation.org).